HARDWOOD

HEROES

GREAT OKLAHOMA
BASKETBALL COACHES

HARDWOOD
HEROES

GREAT OKLAHOMA
BASKETBALL COACHES

BY C. RENZI STONE
& BOB BURKE

SERIES EDITOR: GINI MOORE CAMPBELL
ASSOCIATE EDITOR: ERIC DABNEY

(front cover) Photograph of Sherri Coale is courtesy of University of Oklahoma Athletics. Photographs of Abe Lemons, Henry Iba, Kelvin Sampson, and Bill Self are courtesy of the Oklahoma Publishing Company.

CONTENTS

Famous Oklahoma Coaches

ACKNOWLEDGMENTS

This book was made possible by the help of many people. In developing the list of high school, college, and professional coaches to honor, excellent suggestions were made by Sports Editor Mike Sherman, Berry Tramel, and John Rohde at *The Oklahoman* and Sports Editor Mike Strain and Barry Lewis at the *Tulsa World*.

Photographs were provided by Linda Lynn, Melissa Hayer, Mary Phillips, and Robin Davison at *The Oklahoman*; Justin Lenhart, Museum Director of the Jim Thorpe Association and the Oklahoma Sports Hall of Fame; Crystal Kelso, Sports Information Director at Langston University; Phil Pierce, Assistant Media Relations Director at the University of Arkansas; Mark Brunner, Associate Media Relations Director at the University of Texas at El Paso; Brian Johnson, Assistant Sports Information Director, and Gina Smith at East Central Oklahoma State University; Brian Adler and Justin Tinder, Sports Information Director, at Southwestern Oklahoma State University; Ashley McWilliams, Assistant Media Relations Director at Oral Roberts University; Lindsay Laird and Christen Stark, Director of Public Relations at Northeastern Oklahoma A&M College.

Research assistance was provided by Kasey Hendrix and Mindy Robson at Saxum PR. Our able proofreaders were Glen Johnson, Dan Hays, Mike Houck, and Chuck Bowman. Recollections of life lessons taught and learned were provided by Coach Bill Self, Scott Streller, Desmond Mason, Larry Stone, Coach Kelvin Sampson, Coach Sherri Coale, Coach Eddie Sutton, Eduardo Najera, Kermit Holmes, Coach Dan Hayes, Dan Davis, Jay Mauck, Dante Swanson, and Coach Billy Tubbs.

We are grateful for the excellent work of our editors, Gini Moore Campbell and Eric Dabney.

C. Renzi Stone
Bob Burke
2010

INTRODUCTION

Hustle back on defense! Block your man out!
Pass the ball five times before you shoot!

Even though such basketball phrases cannot be attributed to any one coach, these words of art are heard in gymnasiums across America each day as young men and women of all ages, colors, and socio-economic backgrounds gather to play basketball.

A well-played basketball game in motion, in front of thousands or at a park in front of one onlooker, is a living, breathing symphony and the coach is the maestro. The beauty of the game is how personal it is. Unlike football and baseball, fans, athletes, and coaches in basketball are captured in close quarters to compete—raw emotions for all to see. The story unfolds at a hair-trigger pace before observers and participants alike. It can be crude, intense, and exhausting—all at once. But, when the game is played well, nothing is as exhilarating and beautiful.

The excitement of a basketball game is unmatched in sport. Players make plays, but the coach is ultimately responsible for the game strategy and deciding in a close contest who will take the last shot, or rather who was supposed to take the last shot. Whether the shot goes in or not determines whether that day is praised or mourned in the seconds, minutes, and years later.

Oklahoma has a rich heritage of basketball coaches. The greatest of these men and women fortunately won more games than they lost, yet their legacy is most valued because of their impact on the lives of young men and women they coached. Rarely is a great coach only recognized for wins and losses. In a small state that is nationally recognized for excellence in football, it is basketball that also has a rich tradition of participation and coaching. This is the story of real "Hardwood Heroes"—the great coaches of Oklahoma basketball.

A NEW GAME–
BASKET BALL

The game of basketball is a great example of the old saying "necessity is the mother of invention." In 1891, James Naismith, a Canadian-born physical education instructor at the Young Men's Christian Association (YMCA) in Springfield, Massachusetts, was directed by his superiors to develop a simple, inexpensive game that would keep the boys of the community occupied indoors during the long, harsh New England winter.

Naismith, the son of Scottish immigrants, was given 14 days to come up with a game that was not too rough, did not take up much room, and would help keep his track athletes in shape during the winter. Naismith looked at other popular games of the day including baseball, soccer, hockey, and lacrosse. None could safely be played indoors and each had too much physical contact for his liking.

Naismith met his deadline and wrote 13 basic rules of a new game he called "basket ball." To reduce physical contact, he nailed a peach basket about ten feet from the floor at each end of the gymnasium. His theory was that defending a goal so high in the air would reduce the likelihood that players would slam into each other.

Players used a soccer ball and passed it to each other to move it up the court—dribbling would come decades later. A point was scored if a player shot the ball into the basket. In early years the bottom remained on the basket, so the game had to be stopped for someone to get on a ladder and retrieve the ball. After each goal, a jump ball was held in the middle of the court.

The first official game of "basket ball" was played in December, 1891, with nine boys on each team. There were more fouls than points—the final score was 1-0. Naismith, in his handwritten report of the first game, said most of the fouls were called for running with the ball, although tackling the player with the ball was not uncommon. From the beginning, Naismith recognized that it was important to control the actions of players by calling fouls for improper behavior.

The new game caught on and was recognized internationally by the YMCA in 1893. When looking for a permanent name, Naismith refused attempts to call the game "Naismith Ball." Instead, the game's name gradually became "basketball."

After graduating with a medical degree, Naismith began the men's basketball program at the University of Kansas in 1898. Very few colleges played basketball and Naismith's opponents for the first two decades of Kansas basketball consisted of Haskell Indian Nations

Oklahoma Christian College fans cheer their team to victory in a 1983 game.
Courtesy Oklahoma Publishing Company.

University in Kansas, attended by many Native American students from Indian Territory and Oklahoma Territory, the University of Nebraska, the University of Missouri, and Kansas State University. Ironically, with a record of 55-60, Naismith is the only University of Kansas basketball coach with a losing record.

By 1900 there were enough college teams, primarily on the East Coast, to make intercollegiate basketball competition possible. In 1904, basketball became a demonstration sport at the Olympic Games in St. Louis, Missouri, an amazing feat for a game invented only 13 years before. Basketball became an official sport of the Olympics at the summer games in Berlin, Germany, in 1936.

Americans dominated the sport internationally as highlighted by the 1992 Olympic dream team's sweep of the gold in Barcelona, Spain. However, the world caught up and more people now play the sport globally than any sport besides soccer. Collegiate and professional teams often have international players.

The first men's national basketball championship was organized as the National Association of Intercollegiate Athletics (NAIA) in 1937. The first national championship for larger schools organized in the National Collegiate Athletic Association (NCAA) began with the National Invitation Tournament (NIT) in 1939. The NCAA national tournament began the following year.

High school basketball grew faster than college competition in the first years of the twentieth century. Because many schools across the nation were small and located in rural areas, basketball was an ideal interscholastic sport due to its modest requirements for the number of players and equipment. Frankly, before television coverage promoted college and professional basketball, the popularity of high school basketball was unrivaled in America. Today, nearly every American high school fields a varsity men's and women's basketball team. More than one million high school students represent their schools on the court each year.

Women's basketball began at Smith College in 1892 when Senda Berneson, a physical education instructor, modified Naismith's rules for women. She visited with Naismith, became fascinated by the new sport, and published special rules for women's competition. As editor of a national women's basketball publication, Berneson promoted basketball for female students.

The equipment and technique of basketball have changed dramatically in the past century. When soccer balls gave way to balls made especially for basketball, the balls were brown. It was only in the 1950s that the orange ball came into common use. Dribbling also became a major part of the game in the 1950s as manufacturing improved the ball shape and allowed it to be dribbled easily. In the 120 years since its invention, basketball has become one of the world's most popular team sports, with more than 300 million participants.

Naismith has been honored in many ways for his invention of basketball. The sport's hall of fame is named the Naismith Memorial Hall of Fame in Springfield, the home city of basketball. The NCAA rewards its best players and coaches each year with the Naismith Award. In 2009, University of Oklahoma star Blake Griffin was the Naismith Men's College Player of the Year, a first for a player from Oklahoma.

Basketball is truly an American sport. Although the origins of baseball and football lie in Europe, it was in America that basketball came to life.

BASKETBALL IN OKLAHOMA

asketball came to Oklahoma as early as 1895 at the Oklahoma City YMCA which had been formed shortly after the land run and founding of Oklahoma City in 1889. There was no organized league, but young men and adults who frequented the YMCA programs were introduced to the new sport. Basketball was especially popular during the winter months when Oklahoma winters made it too cold to play baseball or other sports outdoors.

At the beginning of the twentieth century, Oklahoma's schools for Native American youth organized basketball teams for girls and baseball teams for male students. The girls' team at the Euchee Mission in Indian Territory was unbeaten in a three-year period, defeating teams from Tulsa, Claremore, Bristow, Sapulpa, Okmulgee, and Stroud. A newspaper dispatch from Muskogee noted that the strong point of the Euchee Mission team was their team work, "backed up by their swiftness of foot."

The Indian girls played in moccasins instead of shoes. After one game against a much larger team wearing hard shoes, the Euchee Mission players' feet were trampled and bruised, although the Indian girls "were too game to protest." The Euchee team's fame spread and they continued to win games on tours of Missouri and Kansas.

Early Oklahoma schools, both in cities and in rural areas, had little money in their budgets to field competitive sports teams. The state was agrarian with a low tax base. There was hardly enough money to hire teachers and provide ample buildings to educate the children of the growing population, nevertheless buy sports equipment and build venues for sports competition. However, as cities and towns grew, citizens needed a source of pride and school teams helped meet that need.

In 1903, boys and girls basketball was organized at Oklahoma City High School. The captain of the first team was Minnie Partridge, who tragically died the following year from typhoid fever.

The high school teams often played outdoors. In November, 1903, Oklahoma City and Norman played on a Sunday afternoon at Colcord Park in Oklahoma City. A newspaper article noted "a good-sized crowd" witnessed the game. It apparently was a good day for the Norman High School team. The newspaper story said, "It is unnecessary to mention the scores as Oklahoma City is said to have been beaten soundly."

It was not unusual for high school teams to compete against college squads. In December, 1904, *The Daily Oklahoman* featured a game between the Oklahoma City High

School boys and Epworth University, now Oklahoma City University, one of the state's first colleges to form a basketball team. The high school beat the college team 16 to 6. The newspaper reporter wrote:

> It was a fast, clean game, in which science won over brawn. The frequent though unintentional fouling by the high school team was the most unsatisfactory feature of the game, but the Epworth people were unable to take advantage of this on account of their poor throwing of goals.

Before the state's largest colleges began official basketball competition, teacher-training schools in Oklahoma fielded teams. As early as 1904, Southwestern Normal, now Southwestern Oklahoma State University at Weatherford; Northwestern Normal, now Northwestern Oklahoma State University at Alva; and Central Normal, now the University of Central Oklahoma at Edmond; competed against each other and teams from outside Oklahoma, primarily in women's competition. A 1904 newspaper report on happenings at Southwest Normal said, "Grounds have been prepared for basket ball and for tennis. Teams have been formed by the young ladies and we hope to see them sufficiently proficient to play matched games in the near future."

Men's basketball was introduced at the University of Oklahoma (OU) and Oklahoma A & M College, now Oklahoma State University (OSU), in 1907, the year Oklahoma became the 46th state of the Union. Women's basketball, however, was not offered at OSU as an intercollegiate sport until 1973. OU fielded a women's team the following year. Oklahoma was one of the first states to have a major presence of basketball at both large and small colleges and universities.

From 1900 to the 1930s, baseball was king in Oklahoma, in large and small cities and villages alike. Town teams often played to a properly-dressed church crowd on Sunday afternoons. Men from one small town helped civic pride by besting the baseball team from a neighboring town. But as players had less time to devote to town-team sports, junior high school and high school basketball competition rose in popularity.

Basketball soon surpassed baseball as the favorite sport for many school districts. Basketball could be played year round and with fewer players. To help relieve the sedentary life of winter months, small indoor gymnasiums were constructed for basketball. In warm weather, players could participate outside on the school ground or in a neighbor's backyard. There was also no magic number of players needed. Two or three students on each team could play an active game or a sole student could practice his or her shots or make up games such as "horse."

Needing only five players for boys' basketball and six players for a girls' team made the sport popular with small Oklahoma school districts that would have difficulty recruiting enough players to participate in baseball or football competition. The minimal need for equipment was also a factor. School districts often could not afford an expensive football program for its students. But a few inexpensive basketballs and goals allowed students to practice in open-air school yards in preparation for competition with neighboring schools.

Bertha Teague, second from right, and her first girls basketball team at Byng High School in 1927.
Courtesy Oklahoma Publishing Company.

It was basketball, not football or baseball, that produced the first state high school sports champion. In 1918, boys' teams competed in regional competition before playing for the championship in Oklahoma City. The following year, the first unofficial state championship tournament for girls was held. In 1924, the state girls' basketball championship became official.

The early basketball competition was not without controversy and injury. A week before Oklahoma statehood in November, 1907, *The Daily Oklahoman* reported that Raymond Doty of the Epworth University team broke his collarbone during practice. It is the first report of a basketball injury in the pages of the state's largest newspaper. A month later, the newspaper reported on a fist fight that broke out during a scrimmage of Epworth's first and second teams at Convention Hall. The article said, "The affair was adjusted without police interference."

Oklahoma high school girls' basketball has a long tradition. Before 1971 only nine other states offered girls' championship competitions. Bertha Teague, one of the foremost women's coaches in the nation, and future Hall of Famer, started coaching at Byng High School in Pontotoc County in 1927 and won 1,157 games and eight state championships.

Oklahoma was the last state in the nation to eliminate six-on-six girls basketball. In 1987 the Oklahoma Secondary School Activities Association allowed a team to choose between five-on-five and six-on-six. After the 1995 season all high schools converted to the five-on-five game.

In six-on-six, three girls on a team tried to score on one goal, and the other three stayed at the opposite goal, playing defense. None of the girls could cross half-court. Originally, girls had three courts or zones, and the defenders advanced the ball to the centers in the middle of the court and then passed the ball to forwards, who attempted to score. Girls had a limited number of dribbles, could not touch the opposing player, and were not allowed to block shots. In 1939, the rules changed to only two courts, and in 1951 both boys and girls could use the same rules inside those courts.

Public schools were segregated in Oklahoma and most of the nation before the United States Supreme Court case of *Brown v. Board of Education* in 1954. Schools in all-black towns such as Boley and Taft developed great interest in basketball before integration and continued their high level of competition afterwards. Taft won the Class C state championship in boys' basketball three consecutive years in the early 1960s.

Four major Oklahoma colleges and universities have competed in the highest division of the NCAA. Under Coach Bruce Drake, OU won the first Big Six Conference title and made it to the national championship game in 1947. Legendary Coach Henry P. "Hank" Iba guided his Oklahoma A & M team to the national championship in men's basketball in 1945 and 1946, the only Division I state college to ever win the crown. The University of Tulsa and Oral Roberts University are the remaining top-division teams to field men's and women's basketball teams.

Minco's Beth Hailey drives around Angela Cobble of Paden in the 1982 Class A girls state basketball tournament. *Courtesy Oklahoma Publishing Company.*

The nation's oldest college holiday basketball tournament, the All College, is still alive and well. It began in 1936 when Coach Iba and Bus Ham, sports editor of *The Daily Oklahoman*, came up with the idea for a college basketball tournament in Oklahoma City between Christmas and New Year's Day. A small committee of primarily sportswriters for the newspaper invited teams and promised to pay mileage. Immediately, the tournament was flooded with positive responses from coaches who were anxious to play games to ready their squads for conference play. The beneficiary of the first All College Tournament was the Milk and Ice Fund, a benefit that provided milk and ice for disadvantaged children and families.

Small-college basketball has seen great success in Oklahoma. Using primarily players from inside the state, NAIA and NCAA Division II schools have consistently performed well. The Southern Nazarene University (SNU) women's team won five national championships from 1989 to 1998, four consecutively from 1994 to 1997.

The Oklahoma City University (OCU) women won the NAIA crown in 1999, 2000, and 2001. OCU's men's basketball also has been consistently strong. The legendary Abe Lemons coached OCU basketball for 25 years and had 599 career wins, including his time at the University of Texas and Pan-American University. OCU dropped from NCAA Division I basketball to NAIA later and won four national championships in the 1990s, developing great rivalries with Oklahoma Christian College, now Oklahoma Christian University, and Oklahoma Baptist University.

Oklahoma's small-college tradition has an excellent reputation, and the other colleges, as well as junior colleges, all have had competitive teams and have won many championships.

Basketball teams playing under the banner of the Amateur Athletic Union (AAU) are an important part of Oklahoma basketball history. Before the National Basketball Association paid enormous salaries to basketball players, the AAU sanctioned teams fielded by companies such as Phillips Petroleum Company in Bartlesville. The Phillips 66ers were an AAU dynasty, winning six straight national amateur championships from 1943 to 1948, and eight overall. Phillips organized its first basketball team in 1921. Its first star was Paul Endacott, who was the AAU player of the year for Kansas University in 1923. The 66ers attracted top talent, and in 1946 former Oklahoma A&M star Bob Kurland joined the team.

In 1948, five Phillips players played on the gold-medal-winning United States Olympic team coached by 66ers coach Bud Browning. The 66ers era ended in 1968 as professional basketball's popularity soared. Two Oklahoma women's AAU programs, the Presbyterian College Cardinals of Durant and the Tulsa Business School Stenos, won five straight titles in the 1930s.

Although football and baseball have been touted as the sports of Oklahoma, basketball has a strong, rich tradition. The influence of many coaches, including Henry Iba and Bertha Teague, on the sport's national scene is largely underestimated. While not widely recognized like Indiana or North Carolina, Oklahoma has been a strong contributor to the growth of the game in America and basketball remains one of the state's most important sports.

Coach Henry P. Iba with his 1945 national championship basketball team. Front row, left to right, Weldon Kern and Cecil Hawkins. Back row, Doyle Parrack, Coach Iba, Bob Kurland, and Blake Williams. *Courtesy Oklahoma Publishing Company.*

Star Spencer High School's Snake Grensham, center, is upended by Rod Turney of Wakita while David Prater waits to retrieve the errant shot in a 1977 Oklahoma high school All State game. *Courtesy Oklahoma Publishing Company.*

(Facing page) Charles Celestine, right, of Oscar Rose Junior College, and Ray Alford of Seminole Junior College fight for the ball during a 1984 game. *Courtesy Oklahoma Publishing Company.*

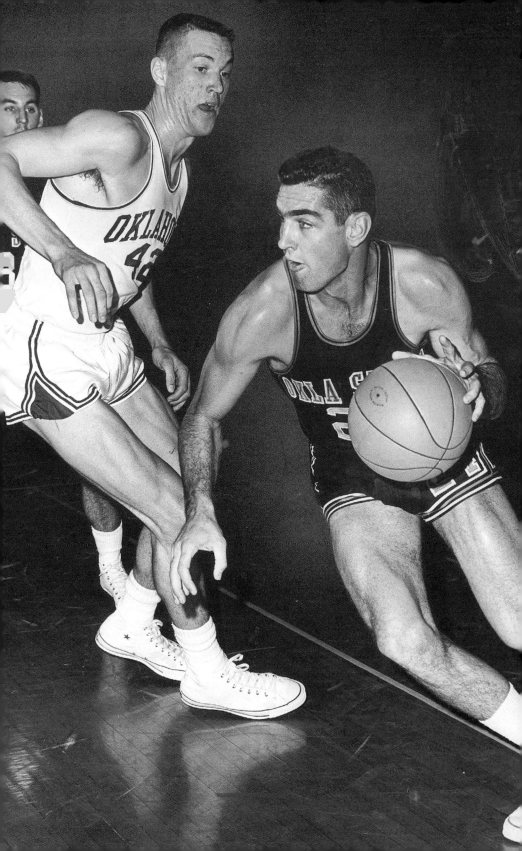

Jump-shooting Shelton White of Moore tries to shoot over Muskogee's Leon Perkins in the first round of the 1972 Class 4A boys basketball tournament. *Courtesy Oklahoma Publishing Company.*

(Facing Page) Oklahoma State University's Cecil Epperley, right, drives around University of Oklahoma Sooner Warren Fouts in a Bedlam Game in Norman in 1962. *Courtesy Oklahoma Publishing Company.*

PROFESSIONAL
BASKETBALL

I n 1988, the Fast Breakers, Tulsa's first professional basketball team, played its inaugural season and won the Continental Basketball Association (CBA) championship. In 1990, the Oklahoma City Cavalry joined Tulsa in the CBA, a developmental association for the NBA. The Fast Breakers left Tulsa in 1992, and the Cavalry developed financial problems and left Oklahoma City in 1997 after winning the championship as well. The Enid Storm joined the United States Basketball League in 2000.

Under the leadership of former sportscaster and Oklahoma City Mayor Mick Cornett, the top level of professional basketball, the National Basketball Association, came to Oklahoma after Hurricane Katrina drove the New Orleans Hornets and owner George Shinn from the New Orleans Arena to a temporary home in Oklahoma City in 2006. The team played at the Ford Center, a professional sports arena built with taxpayer money as part of the MAPS initiative approved by voters in 1993. The Ford Center has recently been renovated as a result of tax money made possible by another vote of the people and serves as a reminder to city leaders that, "If you build it, they will come."

After two seasons, the Hornets returned to New Orleans. In 2008, Oklahoma City became a major league city with the addition of the Oklahoma City Thunder in the NBA. Businessman Clayton I. Bennett and other investors purchased the Seattle Supersonics and, after two seasons in Seattle, moved the franchise to Oklahoma City. Corporate and fan support has exceeded expectations as the entire state has greatly supported the Thunder.

The newest professional basketball franchise in Oklahoma was unveiled in October, 2009, when the Detroit Shock of the WNBA relocated to Tulsa to play in the new downtown arena, the BOK Center. Former University of Tulsa and University of Arkansas coach Nolan Richardson was named the first coach of the Tulsa WNBA team. The Shock had played in Detroit since 1998 and was the first WNBA expansion franchise to win a WNBA championship.

In 2009, Blake Griffin of the University of Oklahoma was the first state player to be named the nation's top collegiate men's basketball player. *Courtesy Oklahoma Publishing Company.*

THE FAST BREAKERS

Co-author C. Renzi Stone's father, Larry Stone, was a transplant to Oklahoma. He had spent a career with Cities Service and when transferred to Tulsa after three previous moves in six years, decided he found his home and left Cities to start his own chain of convenience stores.

The elder Stone had a dream of bringing professional basketball to a city and state still in the depths of the oil bust. The vision became a plan while he was in Kansas City enjoying the 1988 Final Four with his wife. Duke, Arizona, Oklahoma, and Kansas competed. Larry Brown's Jayhawks ultimately upset Billy Tubbs' Sooners 83-79 to win the national championship. Between games, a family friend, Larry Saunders, who played basketball at Duke from 1969 to 1971, told Stone about the near-bankrupt Savannah Spirits of the Continental Basketball Association.

C. Renzi Stone picks up the story:

"You could get them if you wanted," he told Dad. "It wouldn't cost a bunch of money."

"How much," Dad asked?

"Six hundred grand. Maybe less."

"Wow."

And the journey began.

Using profits from Fast Break, his burgeoning convenience store business, my father bought the team and relocated it to Tulsa and named it the Fast Breakers in a marketing move to promote his business. His first act was to hire Henry Bibby, the former New York Knickerbockers great from the 1970s who played with Willis Reed, Kiki Vandeweghe, and others. Bibby beat out future NBA coach Flip Saunders and Cazzie Russell. The next move was to renovate the old Tulsa County Fairgrounds, an old barn of an arena that had seen more FFA and circus events in its lifetime than pro basketball games. Finally, they let Bibby field the team and he rotated 27 players through in year one to find the right mix, a hallmark of managing minor league teams.

The team went 40-27 in that inaugural season and won the league championship prompting a parade in downtown Tulsa attended by thousands. Like any minor league team, the Fast Breakers were led by a bunch of basketball transients, notably Shelton Jones, Terry Faggins, OU great Tim McAllister, former Jayhawk

The 1989 Tulsa Fast Breakers, Oklahoma's first professional basketball team. Front row, left to right, Wes Matthews, Otis Birdsong, Duane Washington, and Dexter Shouse. Back row, Assistant Coach Steve Bontrager, assistant Nolan Richardson, Jr., Tracy Moore, Peter Thibeaux, Michael Graham, Alton Lee Gipson, Ron Spivey, Joe Ward, Coach Henry Bibby, and Trainer Andy Ward.

Cedric Hunter, Ron Spivey, Joe Ward, Duane Washington, Peter Thibeaux, Wes Matthews, Dexter Shouse, and the hometown hero from the University of Tulsa, Tracy Moore.

The success of the team led Stone to look for a rival market to create excitement for fans. Rockford, Illinois and Quad City, South Dakota were hard markets for Tulsans to root against. In 1990, Stone helped a group of investors locate a team in rival market Oklahoma City where the Cavalry would play until shutting down after the 1997 season—the same year the team won the league championship. Years later, Stone would laugh about the games won and lost, but brag about how great it was for Tulsa to win a championship in that first year.

The Fast Breakers would compete for another three seasons in Tulsa, two as the Fast Breakers and one as the Tulsa Zone, under new ownership. The Cavalry and Fast Breakers certainly paved the way for future professional basketball teams in the state.

I am sure that no man can derive more pleasure from money or power than I do from seeing a pair of basketball goals in some out of the way place.

James Naismith

GREAT OKLAHOMA COACHES

AUTHORS' NOTE: Many basketball coaches with Oklahoma connections have excelled at the high school, college, amateur, and professional levels. However, we have chosen to highlight 50 outstanding Oklahoma basketball coaches. To be included in this list, the coach must have been born in Oklahoma or coached in the state for at least 10 seasons.

BILL ALLEN

Born in Tulsa, Allen graduated from Central High School and played collegiate basketball at North Carolina and Colorado. He returned to Tulsa and began working in the oil industry. After volunteering as a coach at the Tulsa Boys Home, he became boys basketball coach at Tulsa Webster High School in 1951.

For the next 25 years, Allen was head coach at Webster, recording 364 victories and winning the state championship in 1966. He coached five high school All Americans and three *Tulsa World* state players of the year. During 24 of his 25 years, he was also Webster's athletic director.

Courtesy Tulsa Webster High School.

In 1972, Allen was inducted into the Oklahoma High School Coaches Hall of Fame, an organization he helped form and was its first president. After retirement from active coaching, he served as a staff member of the Fellowship of Christian Athletes (FCA). Allen helped get FCA off the ground in Oklahoma in 1959. In 2004, he was selected for induction into the National High School Hall of Fame.

Courtesy Oklahoma Publishing Company.

ROBERT E. "BOB" BASS

Bass has coached more levels of basketball than any other Oklahoma coach. He was a successful head coach at the high school level, the NAIA, NCAA, American Basketball Association (ABA), and the National Basketball Association (NBA). With his playing career at Tulsa Will Rogers High School and Oklahoma Baptist University (OBU), Bass' total basketball career exceeds 60 years.

After college, Bass took over a struggling OBU basketball program in 1952. Two years later he realized success, taking the team to the NAIA District 9 playoffs for the next 13 years. He won the district championship six times and advanced to the NAIA National Basketball championship game in 1965, 1966, and 1967. OBU won the title in 1966.

In 1967, Bass became head coach of the Denver Rockets of the newly-organized ABA, taking the team to the playoffs his first two seasons. He then coached at Texas Tech University before returning to the pros as coach of the Miami Floridians and the Memphis Tams. He joined the San Antonio Spurs and coached until 1976 when he moved to the front office, serving in several management positions. In 1995, Bass became general manager and vice president of the Charlotte, and later, New Orleans Hornets. After nine seasons with the team, he retired in 2004.

Courtesy Oklahoma Publishing Company.

NADINE CARPENTER

Carpenter was one of Oklahoma's longest serving basketball coaches, leading the Leflore Savage girls in 43 seasons. When she retired in 1998 with a 821-335 record, she was the state's winningest high school basketball coach and the third-winningest coach in the nation. For her achievements, she was recognized by both houses of the state legislature. She is a member of the Oklahoma Coaches Hall of Fame.

Courtesy University of Oklahoma Athletics.

SHERRI COALE

With a trademark of wearing high heels during games, Coale is ambitious, setting lofty goals for her women basketball players at the University of Oklahoma (OU)—and she has succeeded in meeting those goals. She was born in Healdton, Oklahoma, and graduated from Oklahoma Christian College (OCC) in Oklahoma City in 1987. She played guard on OCC's Lady Eagles basketball team.

Coale's first head coaching job was at Norman High school. After six years, much to the amazement of others, she was chosen to make the huge leap to the college level as head women's basketball coach at the University of Oklahoma in 1997. OU had considered ending the program altogether and many questioned the athletic director's choice of Coale. Steve Owens was serious about OU basketball, but was privately criticized for hiring a high school coach who had never recruited.

Within a few years, Coale brought the Sooners into the national spotlight with an appearance in the national championship game in 2002. In 2005-2006, the Sooners were 16-0 in Big 12 play, only the second team in conference history to go undefeated. In 2009, Coale guided the Sooners to the second round of the NCAA tournament. She had shown the doubters she was for real.

Among Coale's accomplishments at OU are a cumulative team grade point average of 3.0 for 22 consecutive semesters, several Big 12 regular season and tournament championships, and 68 Academic All Americans. She coached Courtney Paris, the most decorated All American women's basketball player from 2005 to 2009, when she was named the National College Women's Player of the Year.

Coale's dominance of women's college hoops has drawn a huge following of fans at Lloyd Noble Arena. When she took over the program, it was fortunate to have 1,500 fans for a game. In 2006, OU women drew more than 12,000 fans to a game against Baylor, the largest crowd to ever see a women's sporting event in Oklahoma.

Coach Sherri Coale, right, celebrates a 2009 NCAA women's college basketball regional tournament final win with Courtney Paris, center, and Jenny Vining. *Courtesy Oklahoma Publishing Company.*

Life Lessons Taught by Coach Coale

I have tried to teach my student-athletes to dream big. I've tried to teach them to expand their ceilings and increase their expectations. Hopefully I've taught them that there are no short cuts, no roads around, no tunnels under. To borrow from Frost, "The best way out is always through." I think they would be able to say they've learned that by doing it.

I think the game teaches them that life isn't always fair, but I've tried to train them to see that they can always choose how they react to it. I've tried to implant in my student-athletes the discipline that is required to do anything well, the necessary combination of confidence and competency in the pursuit of excellence in any endeavor. And that attitude can make up for a whole host of "gifts" that they may think they've been shorted.

I've tried to instill in them a refusal to settle, a mental gauge that drives them to do anything as well as they can possibly do it because it's the right thing to do. I've tried to teach them to pay attention - to the little things and the big things, and especially to people. I hope I've taught them to give back. I've tried to teach them to play for each other, and to do so full throttle, because life was meant to be lived and half-way, in any endeavor, is simply unacceptable. And I sure hope I've taught them to believe."

Life Lessons Learned from Coach Coale

Born in Canada, Stacey Dales was Big Twelve Conference Women's Player of the Year and a first team All American in 2001 and 2002 while leading the Sooners to the national championship game. She played for Washington and Chicago in the WNBA and was a well-known college basketball analyst and ESPN football sideline announcer.

Coach is the kind of mentor that comes around only when the extraordinary is meant to happen. I recall my freshman year, shredding the ACL in my left knee, and Coach sitting with me in the parking lot at my dorm, just listening as I cried. I recall the numerous times that my heart showed just a little too visibly on my sleeve with all of my passion and intensity, and Coach secretly telling me that though she understood, strength was more important at that time.

During my senior year, we became an unquestioned adversary in the Final Four chase. Coach always dreamed big, and her equation of confidence plus passion was infectious. Although we didn't win that last game, something greater was born. Everything that Sherri had ever taught us had manifested itself and come true. It all meant something, finally. Practice was harder than games, and excellence was indeed, an expectation. I can proudly look back and say that we laid a foundation for greatness at the University of Oklahoma. But why shouldn't we? Coach Coale was our leader.

Coach is a mother, leader, and teacher, but mostly for me, she is a blessing. She will always represent this for me. She once told me in a letter, "I'm so glad our paths crossed." Coach, so am I.

Sooner Stephanie Simon Hybl, originally from Clinton, and now married to former OU quarterback Nate Hybl, entered the OU women's basketball program in 1999. As a three-year letter winner, she is remembered by the Sooner family as a natural leader and hard worker with solid offensive skills. While at OU she demonstrated her work ethic and leadership on and off the court.

I think the broader lesson Coach Coale taught about life was the importance of focusing on doing the little things right. By practicing over and over again, you allow yourself to not get overwhelmed by a potentially bigger task at hand – the practice and repetition takes care of the rest. Further, by achieving your goals in a stepwise approach, you don't get bogged down in the sometime arduous process of reaching your end goals. One step at a time truly does lead to victory. These lessons helped me prioritize and balance immediate tasks without losing sight of long-term goals.

Courtesy Oklahoma Publishing Company.

WAYNE COBB

Cobb is the winningest basketball coach in East Central Oklahoma State University history. In 23 seasons, he posted a 417-251 record, won ten conference championships, and took his team to four national tournaments. He coached until January, 2003, when he resigned for health reasons.

In his career, Cobb won 596 games in 32 years at East Central and Murray State College and won another 48 high school games in three years at Sulphur and Chattanooga.

Courtesy Oklahoma Publishing Company.

MIKE DE LA GARZA

De La Garza coached at Oklahoma City Mount St. Mary's High School before taking the boys basketball head coaching job at Edmond in 1976. He fielded championship teams at Edmond for the next 24 years. He led the Bulldogs to their first state championship, the Class 5A title in 1993. At the end of his 30-year coaching career, De La Garza said, "Once you're a basketball coach, you're always a basketball coach. Even without a team now, I still relive the incredible satisfaction to see young men mature and develop not only as individuals but in their careers."

Perhaps De La Garza's most famous player was Bill Self who was Oklahoma's outstanding high school basketball player in 1981. While Self was a star at Edmond Memorial High School three years, De La Garza's teams won 66 games.

BRUCE DRAKE

Drake is a member of the National Basketball Hall of Fame, selected not only because of his coaching success, but also for his work as chairman of the NCAA Rules Committee from 1951 to 1955 and his term as president of the National Basketball Coaches Association. On the court, he developed the "Drake Shuffle" offense and, on the national scene, helped make goal tending illegal. The "Drake Shuffle," called by many as one of basketball's biggest innovations, gave small teams a chance against taller and stronger opponents.

Courtesy Oklahoma Publishing Company.

Growing up in Texas, Drake became a bonafide basketball star at OU. He was a Helms Foundation All American in 1928-1929. He also was a champion pole vaulter and lettered two years as quarterback of the Sooner football team.

Drake was the head men's basketball coach at OU from 1938 to 1955, compiling a 200-181 record. For the decade before assuming the head coach's job, Drake coached the OU basketball freshmen for ten years. In addition to basketball, he coached the golf and swimming teams. After leaving OU, Drake coached the Air Force Academy team to a 34-14 record in 1956-1957.

At OU, Drake made two Final Four appearances, losing to Oregon in 1939 and Holy Cross in 1947. He won or tied for six conference championships in the Big Six and Big Seven conferences.

After his college coaching career, Drake coached the Wichita, Kansas team in the National Industrial Basketball League and was assistant coach of the 1956 United States Olympic basketball team.

In addition to the National Basketball Hall of Fame, Drake was inducted into the Helms Foundation Hall of Fame as a player and coach.

> A winner in basketball is someone who recognizes his God-given talents, works his tail off to develop them into skills, and uses these skills to accomplish his goals.
>
> Bruce Drake

Eddie Evans.
Courtesy Oklahoma Publishing Company.

EDDIE AND TERRY EVANS

This father-son combination is unique in their roles of the basketball program at OU and the University of Central Oklahoma (UCO). Eddie was an All State player at Oklahoma City's Douglass High School, coached two high school state championship teams, and was head men's coach at UCO from 1978 until 1992. He was comfortable in his coaching role and brought his young son, Terry, to most practices, team meetings, and on road trips.

With his father as his model, Terry was a member of three state basketball championship teams at Millwood High School and started all four years at OU, receiving Player of the Year honors on the Academic All Big Eight squad three times. He coached high school basketball at Chickasha and won three state championships in four years at Midwest City High School.

In 2002, Terry became head basketball coach at UCO and led the Bronchos to five national tournament appearances in his first eight years.

Terry Evans, left, drives to a basket in the 1993 NIT Tournament. *Courtesy Oklahoma Publishing Company.*

The invention of basketball was not an accident.
It was developed to meet a need. Those boys simply
would not play "Drop the Handkerchief."

James Naismith

Courtesy Oral Roberts University.

JERRY FINKBEINER

Finkbeiner put together a string of three NAIA women's national championships at his alma mater, Southern Nazarene University (SNU), before beginning a long run at Oral Roberts University.

A native of southern California, Finkbeiner was an All-American at SNU in 1978. He coached the women's basketball team at SNU from 1990 to 1996. Winning three consecutive titles, SNU had a 99-4 record from 1994 to 1996. He was named the NAIA National Coach of the Year in 1994, 1995, and 1996.

In 1996, Finkbeiner was named women's coach at ORU and has taken the program to new heights. In the ten years prior to his hiring, ORU had only 85 total wins and two winning seasons. In the 13 years since, Finkbeiner has led the Golden Eagles to more than twice that number of victories with the first five appearances at the NCAA tournament for the women's team in school history.

VARRYL "CHOP" FRANKLIN

Franklin, an Oklahoma City native, is the state's most successful high school basketball coach in the number of state championships won, 11, a feat unmatched in basketball with the probable exception of the late Red Auerbach who won 16 NBA championships as a coach and front-office executive. Franklin has seven other state titles as an assistant coach in basketball and football.

Courtesy Oklahoma Publishing Company.

After graduating from Lincoln University in Missouri, Franklin returned to Oklahoma City and looked for a job at his alma mater, Douglass High School. However, there were no openings so he took a job as an assistant football coach at Millwood High School in 1973. Soon he assumed control of the Millwood basketball program and began producing district and state champions at an unprecedented rate.

Franklin created a style that is distinctly Millwood's. A sportswriter wrote, "The Falcons trap and hound and wear down their opponents. They use a dozen players or more, Franklin subbing them in like hockey shifts."

Franklin is called the "Minister of Millwood" because of his legendary relationship with players, past and present. His grandfather established a Baptist church in northeast Oklahoma City and Franklin continues the tradition of trying to live a good example for his players.

Courtesy Langston University Sports Information Department.

CAESAR "ZIP" GAYLES

Gayles was an All American in football and basketball at Morehouse College in Atlanta, Georgia, where he graduated in 1924. He later was named to the school's All-Star team for the first half of the twentieth century. After graduation, he coached and taught at Tennessee A & I and Arkansas A & M colleges.

In 1930, Gayles became head football, baseball, and basketball coach and athletic director at Langston University. In 36 years at Langston, he carved a permanent place for himself in American athletic history. In basketball, he guided Langston to a 571-281 record. From 1944 to 1946, his basketball teams won 51 games in a row. He won or tied ten Southwestern Athletic Conference championships and two National Negro championships. In March, 1946, Langston became the first and only college team to beat the Harlem Globetrotters.

Gayles was a strict disciplinarian. No matter how good the player was, he showed no favoritism. He once threatened to bench Marques Haynes because of his fancy dribbling. Haynes later became famous as a member of the Harlem Globetrotters as the "world's greatest dribbler."

The Langston University gymnasium is named for Gayles who is a member of the Oklahoma Sports Hall of Fame and the NAIA Basketball Coaches Hall of Fame.

JOE GILBERT

When Gilbert began coaching basketball at Barnsdall High School in 1954, he fully intended to stay only a couple of years and move on to a larger town. However, he fell in love with the Osage County community and has stayed for more than 50 years. He was still coaching in 2009.

By his own count, in 55 years, Gilbert has won 3,362 games in six varsity sports. He won 812 games in girls basketball and 649 games in boys competition.

Courtesy Barnsdall High School.

A coach is someone who can give correction
without causing resentment.

John Wooden

Courtesy Oklahoma Publishing Company.

PAUL HANSEN

Hansen was a coach for more than 40 years in which he posted a 686-374 record. After coaching prep basketball at Noble Junior High School and Jackson Junior High School in Oklahoma City, he served as an assistant to Coach Abe Lemons at Oklahoma City University for 18 years. Hansen and Lemons had played together at OCU.

In 1974, Hansen replaced Lemons as head coach at OCU and led the Chiefs for six seasons. From 1980 to 1986, he was head men's coach at Oklahoma State University. In 1981, his second season, the Cowboys were 18-9 and Hansen was named Big Eight Conference Coach of the Year. In 1983, OSU was 27-7.

In 1987, Hansen was hired as head basketball coach at the University of Science and Arts (USAO) in Chickasha. Ironically, he died in 1993 on the day that his good friend, Henry Iba, was buried in Stillwater. Hansen is a member of the Oklahoma Sports Hall of Fame.

When Hansen died, longtime sportswriter Frank Boggs said, "He was as close to perfect as you could get. His whole lifetime was spent around champions, seeing champions. The thought never occurred to him that he was the best one of them all."

Courtesy Oklahoma Publishing Company.

JACK HARTMAN

Born in Dewey, Oklahoma, and raised in Shidler, Hartman played basketball and football at Oklahoma State University. He played quarterback in the Canadian Football League before he became an assistant basketball coach in 1954 at OSU. He was head men's basketball coach at Coffeyville Community College in Kansas for seven years and eight years at Southern Illinois University.

In 1970, Hartman began a 16-year stint as head coach at Kansas State University. At KSU, he won 294 games and finished in first or second place in 10 of the 16 seasons in the Big Eight Conference. After his retirement, he was a color commentator for KSU basketball. He died in 1998.

Hartman was Big Eight Conference Coach of the Year in 1975 and 1977. He was named National Coach of the Year by the Associated Press in 1981.

Courtesy Oklahoma Publishing Company.

NATE HARRIS

Harris became the men's basketball coach at Booker T. Washington High School in Tulsa in 1983. His first season ended with a loss in the state championship game against Oklahoma City's John Marshall High School.

After 25 years at Washington, Harris retired in 2007. He won ten state championships and recorded 632 victories. He also lost in five title games, making him the high school coach to lead his team to the most state championship games. Harris coached many future professional athletes including R.W. McQuarters, Etan Thomas, and Ryan Humphrey.

DON HASKINS

Donald Lee Haskins was born in Enid, Oklahoma, and earned All-State honors in basketball and baseball at Enid High School. At Oklahoma A & M, he lettered three years and played on Henry Iba-coached teams that went to the Final Four twice.

Haskins graduated from A & M in 1952. He coached at three high schools in Texas before becoming head basketball coach at Texas Western University, now the University of Texas at El Paso (UTEP) in 1961. In 38 years, Haskin's UTEP teams won 719 games, a national championship, and seven Western Athletic Conference (WAC) titles. He also led his team to 14 NCAA Tournament appearances and appeared in the NIT seven times. He had only four losing seasons.

Courtesy University of Texas at El Paso.

The highlight of Haskins' career was the 1966 national championship game when UTEP's all-black lineup upset the highly-favored all-white lineup of the University of Kentucky. After winning the crown, Haskins said, "It's no big deal." A movie, "Glory Road," was made of the events surrounding the famous tournament.

For his gruff demeanor and prowling the sideline, Haskins earned the nickname "The Bear." After a heart attack and triple bypass surgery, he retired from UTEP in 1999. He was an assistant coach to Henry Iba at the 1972 Olympic Games. He is a member of the Naismith Memorial Basketball Hall of Fame, the Texas Sports Hall of Fame, and the Oklahoma Sports Hall of Fame.

Courtesy Oklahoma Publishing Company.

Dan Hays

Hays grew up in Albuquerque, New Mexico, and earned a degree from Eastern New Mexico University. After coaching high school basketball in Grants and Roswell, New Mexico, he was an assistant coach at Eastern Washington University. In 1975, he came to Oklahoma as an assistant coach at Southeastern Oklahoma State University. He was head coach at Northwestern Oklahoma State University from 1978 to 1983, when he was hired as basketball coach at Oklahoma Christian College, now Oklahoma Christian University.

Hays has the most collegiate wins of any active coach in Oklahoma and is third all-time to Bloomer Sullivan and Henry Iba. Hays captured his 600th college victory in a November, 2008, game against Hillsdale Free Will Baptist College. At the beginning of the 2009 season, he was approaching 700 victories. He is a member of the NAIA Hall of Fame and is the winningest coach in Oklahoma Christian history.

Hays has seen more than 60,000 youth attend his basketball cage camp at Oklahoma Christian each summer. The camp started with meager beginnings but has developed into a well-respected training ground for potential basketball players.

Life Lessons Taught by Coach Hays

Everything is about respect. Respect your education and get your degree. Respect your family and do the right thing. Nothing good happens after midnight. Respect what ability you have on the court and be the best your talent will allow.

Life Lessons Learned from Coach Hays

From Calera, Oklahoma, Jay Mauck was an undersized guard at 5'7". Not highly recruited because of his size, Jay gave an "outsized" effort for the Eagles.

There was a time after Coach Hays had back surgery that he was in so much pain that most people would have just stayed in bed, but he still made it to practice. When the pain got too bad, he coached us lying flat on his back, whistle in his mouth. When you see your coach give that much, you never want to let him down. His devotion to the team made us even more willing to give our best for him and for the team.

He also taught us to be prepared for every situation. Our scouting walk-throughs seemed to last forever. Coach Hays would go over all the opponents' plays and stats for each player on the board in the locker room, and then we would walk through the plays on the court. At the time we dreaded it, but when it came time to face our opponent, we were totally prepared. We knew all their plays, we knew which players could shoot, and which ones we could foul. Preparation gave us an edge on the competition and confidence in our ability to defeat them.

Courtesy Oklahoma Publishing Company.

CHARLES HEATLY

Heatly grew up on a farm in the community of Reed, 12 miles west of Mangum, before attending college at Central State College, now the University of Central Oklahoma. He graduated from Central State in 1956 and coached at Carter, Oklahoma, before settling in Lindsay for the next four decades. Heatly coached girls and boys basketball. He excelled with his girls teams, winning two state championships and was runner-up three other times.

However, Heatly's legacy to Oklahoma basketball is his summer camps. When he attended a tiny camp in Eufaula one summer, he knew he could produce a better summer environment for girls wanting to improve their skills. For the next 26 years, Heatly and volunteers moved furniture from the classrooms at Lindsay High School and moved in beds for the Lindsay Basketball Camp. More than 55,000 girls went through the camp. It was not unusual to have 300 girls per week for nine weeks in the summer.

LOU HENSON

Henson was born in Okay, Oklahoma, and graduated from college at New Mexico State University after attending junior college in Oklahoma at Connors State College. He began his coaching career at Las Cruces High School in New Mexico and won three state championships in his four years there.

In 1962, Henson moved to the college ranks as head basketball coach at Hardin-Simmons University. Four years later, he became head coach at his alma mater, New Mexico State. In 1970, Henson led the Aggies to the Final Four for the only time in school history. The Aggies played in the NCAA tournament six of his nine seasons.

In 1975, Henson was hired as head coach at the University of Illinois and became the school's winningest coach with 423 victories in 21 seasons. He came out of retirement to coach New Mexico State again from 1997 to 2005. He completed his career with 779 victories, sixth on the all-time list.

Henson is considered by supporters of Illinois basketball to be the most beloved basketball coach in the school's history.

Courtesy University of Illinois.

Courtesy Oklahoma Publishing Company.

BARRY HINSON

Currently the Director of External Relations at the University of Kansas, Hinson was born in Marlow, Oklahoma. He was an assistant high school basketball coach at Stillwater and Edmond before becoming head coach at Bishop Kelley High School in Tulsa in 1987. In 1993, he was hired as an assistant coach at Oral Roberts University. In 1997, he took the head coaching job and led the golden Eagles for two seasons.

In 1999, Hinson became head basketball coach at Southwest Missouri State University, now Missouri State University. He led his team to four appearances in the NIT Tournament in nine seasons.

In 2008, he became an administrative assistant for Coach Bill Self at Kansas. Many years before, he was Self's assistant coach at Edmond Memorial High School.

HENRY IBA

Arguably one of basketball's most famous coaches, Henry Payne Iba was born in Missouri and began his coaching career at Oklahoma City's Classen High school. In two years, his team was 51-5 and won the state championship in 1928 and 1929. He coached at Maryville Teachers College in Missouri and the University of Colorado before taking over the Oklahoma A & M basketball program in 1935.

At Stillwater, Iba won 655 games and lost 316 for a .675 percentage. He also coached baseball until 1941 and assumed the job of athletic director less than a year after he arrived on campus.

Coach Henry P. Iba with his 1945 national championship basketball team. *Courtesy Oklahoma Publishing Company.*

Iba's Cowboys won the NCAA national men's basketball championship in consecutive years, 1945 and 1946, led by Bob Kurland, college basketball's first big man. The Cowboys beat New York University in 1945 and the University of North Carolina in 1946. Iba was named National Coach-of-the-Year in both seasons. He also led the United States Olympic team to gold medals in 1964 and 1968 and a silver medal in 1972. In all, Iba won 767 college games.

Known as the "Iron Duke," Iba's basketball teams were famous for their tough, man-to-man defenses and the "Iba deep freeze," holding the ball for the final minutes of a close game. In his later years, Iba had no problem in adjusting to major changes in the game, including the jump shot and bonus free throws.

Iba is perhaps indirectly responsible for T. Boone Pickens' $165 million donation to OSU's athletic program. In the 1950s, Pickens was an unemployed OSU graduate looking for a job and asked Iba for help. The coach set up Pickens with interviews for high school basketball coaching jobs. Even though he did not become a coach, Pickens never forget the favor and said it provided impetus for his donation. Pickens said, "Mr. Iba would be very happy with my performance."

Courtesy Oklahoma Publishing Company.

Iba is a member of the Naismith Memorial Basketball Hall of Fame, the Oklahoma Hall of Fame, the Oklahoma Sports Hall of Fame, the Missouri Hall of Fame, and the Helms Foundation All-Time Hall of Fame.

Taking Care of Mr. Iba

We spend so much time talking about the impact coaches make on players while they are playing, we often forget about how these giants shape the lives of those around them, including student managers, graduate assistants, and friends. Henry P. Iba was one of the great coaches in Oklahoma history as measured by wins and losses, but he was also a terrific citizen, friend, and mentor.

Scott Streller of Oklahoma City was a graduate assistant hired by Eddie Sutton in the fall of 1990. One of Streller's tasks, in Coach Eddie Sutton's words, was to "take care of Mr. Iba." Streller related a few of the priceless stories.

As our relationship developed and he began to trust and get to know me, he would let me help him with more of his daily activities. At 86, he was aging well and was still sharp, but was noticeably slower getting around each year. I would help him go through his mail, take him to the doctor, or just run an errand. Mainly, I took him to practice every day if he was up for it. It was common for a famous coach such as Bobby Knight or Don Haskins to call before we left for the day. Mr. Iba loved Eddie Sutton. After he was named coach, Mr. Iba often repeated how proud he was that one of his boys had come home to run the program. It was a special time, like a family reunion feel, and at the same time a feeling that success was in the near future. It brought Mr. Iba great joy and peace in his last few years to see the program that he had spent so many years building reaching national prominence again.

I drove Mr. Iba around town to wherever he wanted to go. It was like Driving Miss Daisy. The car I used was then-assistant coach Bill Self's school car (Ford Taurus). After the first game, I was driving Mr. Iba to his home five miles outside of town and realized Bill's car was low on gas. We had passed the one gas station and Mr. Iba was very tired so I figured we could get to his home and then I would get gas on the way back to campus. Sure enough, we ran out of gas about 400 yards from the entrance to Mr. Iba's neighborhood on a sleepy two-lane road. There was only one car in sight a ways back from us. Mortified at the situation, I jumped out and stood in the middle of the road and pleaded for help.

Thankfully they were big OSU fans. I explained frantically that I was in Bill Self's car and had Mr. Iba in the back seat in need of getting home. Mr. Iba knew this young kid had just run out of gas, but he was always a gentleman and did not give me a hard time. I felt like a big enough idiot on my own. Coach Sutton and I had many laughs through the years about running out of gas on a cold November night with a feeble Mr. Iba in the car. I made sure Bill knew that I was upset about the gas situation and urged him to keep the car full.

I was responsible for making certain Mr. Iba made it to practice and positioned him with a front row seat to evaluate the action. I wrote down anything he said and prepared a report for Coach Sutton and the assistant coaches for the

I never pretended to be a good loser.
I was a gracious loser, yes, but if you are a good loser,
you might make a habit of it.

Henry P. Iba

next day's coaches meeting. There were many times that first season that Coach Sutton would come over to press row and consult with Mr. Iba since there was such a transition from the previous year's team and coaches. More amazing than my great fortune to hear the conversations between these two legends was the fact that the Cowboys were co-champions of the Big Eight Conference.

The second season Mr. Iba was still very involved, but his health was beginning to fail. We had a freshman named Bryant Reeves who we all believed was a big project who might be able to play by the time he was a junior. We had every intention of redshirting Bryant, who had not yet been named "Big Country." Mr. Iba noticed immediately how "great his hands were." We had been practicing for only a week when Mr. Iba told me, "That big freshman is getting better fast." Mr. Iba still had such a great mind and eye for talent. The player he liked in week one became Big Eight Player of the Year as a sophomore and later led the Cowboys to the Final Four in 1995.

Once Mr. Iba huddled with all coaches in the OSU locker room for a strategy session. I distinctly remember Assistant Coach Rob Evans asking this question, "Mr. Iba, If you could put one quality on what makes a coach successful what would it be?" Mr. Iba, 86 years young, raised his coffee mug to his mouth in deep thought. Finally, he looked Rob directly in the eye with those powerful eyes and said, "SINCERITY! Kids know when you are sincere." We scribbled his words down as if they had come from on high.

Courtesy Oklahoma Publishing Company.

JOHNNIE JOHNSON

Johnson took over a mediocre basketball program at Star Spencer High School in 1974, endured two losing seasons, then built a program that draws few comparisons. In 1976, he led the Bobcats to their first state championship, the first of four in a row, and seven overall. In the 22 years following Star Spencer's first appearance, the team missed the state tournament only four times.

When Johnson retired in 1997, his record over 24 years was 478-156, with four seasons with more than 20 victories. He was *The Daily Oklahoman* coach of the year in 1976 and Big All-City Coach of the Year in three other seasons.

Johnson believed his biggest problem was to convince players to be good citizens. He said, "I had to motivate them to be a student and good person first, then we'd be able to play ball. My first year, I cut 13 seniors."

After retirement from coaching, Johnson continued to reach kids as pastor of St. Mark Baptist Church in Oklahoma City.

Courtesy Oklahoma Publishing Company.

ABE LEMONS

When Lemons was born in Ryan, Oklahoma, he was given the initials-only name "A.E." But after graduating from nearby Walters, Oklahoma, High School in 1941, he joined the Merchant Marine and changed his name to Abe. After military service, Lemons played basketball at Southwestern State Teachers College, now Southwestern Oklahoma State University, and Oklahoma City University.

Lemons always wanted to be a coach and was one of college basketball's premier major college coaches from 1955 to 1990. He won 599 games at OCU from 1955 to 1973, Pan American University from 1973 to 1976, the University of Texas from 1976 to 1982, and again at OCU from 1983 to 1990. He produced many All-American players and became the game's most quoted coach. At the end of the twentieth century, *USA Today* chose one of Lemon's famous lines, "Doctors bury their mistakes—ours are still on scholarship," as the sports quote of the century.

Beneath his funny-man exterior, Lemons was an outstanding coach. He was recognized as a brilliant offensive coach in an era of high-scoring college basketball. However, his players regarded him as much more than a basketball coach. All-American Arnold Short said, "He took me as a boy and made me into a man. He taught me the value of life and friendship."

Diagnosed with Parkinson's Disease, Lemons retired from OCU in 1990. In 2000, the university named its new basketball court "Abe Lemons Arena." Lemons is a member of the Oklahoma Sports Hall of Fame and the Oklahoma Hall of Fame.

Finish last in your league and they call you idiot. Finish last in medical school and they call you doctor.

Abe Lemons

Life Lessons Taught by Coach Lemons

Every lesson I taught players about basketball applied to life. Sure, I wanted a championship team, but it was more important to me that players graduated and led successful lives. I wanted them to always keep a good mental attitude. Even if we didn't win, I wanted them to play reputable ball so we could look people in the eye the next day.

I could tell everything about a kid from his attitude. I wanted players who would accept instruction and be willing to be both a good student in the classroom and a hard-working player on the basketball court. I asked them what was important in their life? If their immediate answer was about material things, I made it a habit to try to direct their learning experience toward the things that really counted, family and friends.

Players need correction, but humor can make them remember it, rather than hate it. Once when a player complained in the cafeteria about having a bad cold, I shot back, "That's probably from the draft from all them ol' boys rushin' past you with the ball."

Life Lessons Learned from Coach Lemons

Dan Davis is one of hundreds of former OCU and University of Texas players who fondly remember "life lessons" uniquely taught by Coach Lemons. After college and law school, Davis became a successful lawyer in Oklahoma City.

Some days, Coach Lemons talked more about life than about basketball. He never came down hard on players even when we messed up. If we missed class, he calmly warned us that it would catch up with us later in life.

One day before practice, Coach Lemons called us together in the old Frederickson Fieldhouse. He wanted to expound on the issue of always doing the right thing and abiding by the rules.

Coach said there were two kinds of rules. There were university rules, rules that students had to obey in order to prevent expulsion from school. The second type of rules was society's rules—if you violate those you go to jail.

Coach told us we must obey both or risk certain punishment. At a quiet time in the meeting, he said, "You take Mr. Davis here. He did not follow the rules of the University and has been asked to move off campus." I had conveniently forgotten that students of the opposite gender were not allowed in our dorm after hours. But Coach Lemons said, "I gave Mr. Davis back his scholarship because I believe in second chances, especially when that person who needs a second chance can shoot a jump shot!"

That was the way Coach Lemons was. He had a heart as big as Oklahoma, the state he loved so much.

JOHN LOFTIN

Loftin graduated from West Texas State University and coached at Murray State College in Tishomingo from 1975 to 1981. After his time at Murray, he began an amazing run of success at Southwestern Oklahoma State University (SWOSU).

Loftin was head women's basketball coach at SWOSU for 19 seasons from 1981 to 2000. He posted an overall record of 499-99, 83.4 %. He won five NAIA national championships in 1982, 1983, 1985, 1987, and 1990. His Lady Bulldog team made ten appearances in the Final Four of the NAIA National Tournament. Loftin coached 11 different first team NAIA All Americans at SWOSU, including Kelli Litsch, a member of the Women's Basketball Hall of Fame.

Courtesy Southwestern Oklahoma State University.

Courtesy Oklahoma Publishing Company.

LEROY "BONEY" MATTHEWS

The old Purcell High School gymnasium was named for Matthews who began coaching boys basketball at Purcell in 1945. By the time he retired in 1973, the Hall of Fame coach had amassed 627 wins, giving him 922 wins in his career at Oklahoma high schools. He won three state championships at Purcell in 1950, 1957, and 1961.

Not just a legendary coach, Matthews still holds the state, and perhaps, the world record for touchdowns scored in a game. In a 1927 game, Matthews scored 14 touchdowns and 14 extra points for his Roff High School football team in a 142-0 victory over Lehigh.

Courtesy East Central Oklahoma
State University.

MICKEY McBRIDE

A member of the NAIA Hall of Fame and the Oklahoma Coaches Association Hall of Fame, McBride coached men's basketball at East Central Oklahoma State University (ECU) in Ada from 1927 to 1967 with a four-year break due to military service in World War II. His career coaching record was 601-253, including a 412-253 mark at ECU.

McBride won nine conference championships at ECU and tied for another. At one point, his team won five consecutive conference championships and 46 straight games. He took six teams to the NAIA National Tournament and another three squads to the National AAU Tournament.

ECU fans believe 1949-1950 is perhaps McBride's best season. The Tigers, behind two All-Americans, Claudell Overton and Stacey Howell, posted a 33-3 record and advanced to the championship game of the NAIA National Tournament. In 1930, McBride's team finished third in the national tournament.

Courtesy Oklahoma Publishing Company.

SHELBY METCALF

Metcalf grew up in Tulsa and graduated from Central High School. He was an All-American guard at East Texas State University where he led his team to three NAIA national tournaments, winning the NAIA crown his senior season.

In 1958, Metcalf became freshman basketball coach at Texas A & M University. Five years later, in 1963, he became head coach, a position he held for 27 seasons until his retirement in 1990. He won more games than any other coach in the old Southwest Conference and is the longest serving basketball coach in conference history. His career collegiate coaching record was 438-306. He was known as "The King of Tournaments" for taking the Aggies to 74 in-season tournaments to make certain his team would play at least one game each year on a neutral floor.

At Texas A & M, Metcalf won six conference championships and made five NCAA tournament appearances.

JOHN NOBLES

In 27 years as a girls basketball coach, Nobles won more than 80 percent of his games with a lifetime record of 588-136. He coached three state champions, four state runners-up, 15 area champions, 21 regional champions, and 10 district champions.

When the debate raged in the 1980s over whether to scrap girls 6-on-6 in favor of the more modern 5-on-5 style of play, Nobles was one of the leading voices to keep the old style. Jim Peck of Woodward, Jay Sherry of Chickasha, and Nobles lobbied for the right for schools to choose which brand of girls basketball to play. When the Oklahoma Secondary School Activities Association voted to ban six-on-six competition, Nobles said, "It's a shame that people are going to be forced to do something they don't want to do. We're not trying to keep anyone from playing 5-on-5. We just want to preserve the freedom of choice."

Nobles' final state championship was in 1989 when an illegible player during the season caused officials to force the Lady Lions to forfeit 14 games. The forfeits did not affect Nobles' team from beating Mustang 44-36 in the Class 5A state final.

In 1989, Nobles was named the national girls basketball coach of the year by Wilson Sporting Goods Company.

Courtesy Oklahoma Publishing Company.

Courtesy Oklahoma Publishing Company.

BENNIE OWEN

Owen was born in Chicago and was a football star at the University of Kansas. He became head football coach at the University of Oklahoma in 1905. Two years later, weeks before Oklahoma became a state, he organized a basketball team. For 13 seasons, he guided the Sooners basketball program to three conference championships, two undefeated seasons, and had only two losing seasons.

Owen's basketball coaching career was overshadowed by his success in football. He introduced the forward pass in the Southwest and was a charter member of the College Football Hall of Fame. OU's football playing field is named for Owen who died in 1970 at the age of 95.

TED OWENS

A native of Hollis, Oklahoma, Owens is the third-winningest basketball coach in University of Kansas history, behind Phog Allen and Roy Williams.

Owens was a three-year basketball letterman at the University of Oklahoma from 1949 to 1951. His first coaching job was at Cameron State Junior College in Lawton. In four seasons, his teams never won less than 20 games and three times advanced to the national junior college tournament semifinals. At Cameron, Owens had a 93-24 record and coached four junior college All-Americans.

In 1960, Owens became an assistant basketball coach at Kansas and was promoted to head coach after the 1963-1964 season. In 19 seasons until this retirement in 1983, Owens posted a 348-182 record for the Jayhawks. He was named Big Eight Coach of the Year five times and National Coach of the Year in 1978 by *Basketball Weekly*. He coached five All-Americans including Jo Jo White and Darnell Valentine. His 1971 and 1974 Jayhawk teams advanced to the Final Four and his 1968 team lost to Dayton in the finals of the National Invitation Tournament (NIT).

Courtesy Jim Thorpe Association.

After he retired, Owens coached high school basketball at Metro Christian Academy in Tulsa. In 2009, he was inducted into the Oklahoma Sports Hall of Fame and the Kansas Sports Hall of Fame.

Courtesy Oklahoma Publishing Company.

DOYLE PARRACK

Born in Cotton County, Oklahoma, Parrack played basketball at Oklahoma A & M and was part of the national championship team in 1945. He played one season for the Chicago Stags of the NBA then became head men's basketball coach at Oklahoma City University.

Parrack led OCU from a team without a gym or scholarships to membership in the NCAA and four consecutive trips to the NCAA tournament. Two of his players, Abe Lemons and Paul Hansen, later coached at OCU.

After eight years at OCU, Parrack was named head men's coach at the University of Oklahoma in 1955. In 1962, Parrack became an assistant to his mentor, Coach Henry Iba, at OSU. Parrack later coached the Israel national basketball team.

Parrack is a member of the sports halls of fame at OCU, OSU, and OU.

LUTHER PEGUES

A member of the Oklahoma Coaches Association Hall of Fame, Pegues led Tulsa McClain High School to the boys basketball state tournament 10 times in 13 seasons from 1993 to 2005. Prior to that, he coached the McClain girls team to six appearances in the state tournament.

Pegues was the first black basketball player at the University of Pittsburgh, graduated with an engineering degree, and was a weather forecaster in the Air Force.

In addition to his many years of coaching, Pegues is known for founding the Pig's Pop-Off, an annual tournament at McLain High School that grew to be the largest summer basketball tournament in the Tulsa area. Past and present NBA players who have played in the tournament are Moses Malone, Karl Malone, Dennis Rodman, Larry Johnson, and John Starks.

Courtesy McClain High School.

Courtesy Oklahoma Publishing Company.

BOB PIGG

Many observers called Pigg the king of girls basketball in Oklahoma in the 1980s. After he retired from the Air Force in 1975, he began his second career building a girls basketball dynasty at Mustang High School. The Broncos were 349-83 during Pigg's 16 seasons.

In the 1980s, Pigg led his team to the state finals seven times and won four state championship crowns. He was named National Girls Basketball Coach of the Year in 1991.

During the 1980s controversy over staying with 6-on-6 girls basketball, Pigg surprised some fellow coaches by enthusiastically supporting the switch to 5-on-5 competition.

DENNY PRICE

Price was a successful basketball player and coach, but was best known in his later years as the father of basketball superstars Mark and Brent Price. However, the elder Price was part of the best fast break high school squad in the state, according to Ray Soldan, who covered prep sports in Oklahoma for nearly 50 years. In 1955, Price led the Norman Tigers to the state Class AA title. He still holds the record for most points in a big-school state tournament game—42—equaled only by his son, Mark, in 1982.

Courtesy Oklahoma Publishing Company.

After playing college basketball at OU, Price landed a position at Phillips University in Enid, Oklahoma, where he coached, at various times, mens and womens basketball and golf and was the athletic director. He coached men's basketball from 1986 to 1993 and led the women's team through 1996. Price, known as one of the nation's preeminent basketball shooting instructors, coached the Oklahoma Storm, a professional team based in Enid, to the United States Basketball League title game. The YMCA in Enid is named for Price.

*Courtesy University of Arkansas
Athletic Media Relations.*

NOLAN RICHARDSON

Born in Texas, Richardson played college basketball at Texas Western College, now the University of Texas at El Paso, During his senior year, he played for former OSU great Don Haskins. After a decade of coaching high school basketball in Texas, Richardson became head coach at West Texas Junior College where he won the National Junior College championship in 1980. From 1981 to 1985 he was head coach at the University of Tulsa. The Golden Hurricane won the NIT in 1981.

In 1985 Richardson moved to the head coaching job at the University of Arkansas where took the Razorbacks to the Final Four three times, losing to Duke in the semifinals in 1990, winning the national championship in 1994 against Duke, and losing in the championship game to UCLA in 1995. He was named National Coach of the Year in 1994.

After serving as head coach of the Panamanian National Team and the Mexican National Team, Richardson was named head coach of the Tulsa WNBA franchise in 2009. He is the only coach to win the NIT and the national championship in the junior college and Division I levels of competition.

Courtesy Oklahoma Publishing Company.

HENRY ROLAND

When Roland took his Beggs High School Demons to the state championship game in March, 1993, it was his ninth appearance in the finals and his sixth title. He also won championships in 1972 and 1973 at Sasakwa and in 1980 at Konawa.

In the 1993 Class 3A finals, Beggs exploded for 23 points in the final quarter to win by five points at the State Fair Arena in Oklahoma City.

Courtesy Oklahoma Publishing Company.

KELVIN SAMPSON

Sampson was born in Pembroke, a Lumbee Native American community in North Carolina, where he excelled in sports and played for his father at Pembroke High School. He completed his education at Pembroke State University and Michigan State University where he earned a master's degree and spent a year as a graduate assistant in basketball at the same time Magic Johnson was a Spartan.

He coached five seasons at Montana Tech University where he won three Frontier Conference championships. In 1986 he was named assistant coach at Washington State University and took over the top job in 1988 for the Cougars. In his final season at Washington State, 1994, Sampson led the Cougars to their first NCAA tournament appearance in 11 years.

Sampson became the 11th coach at the University of Oklahoma in 1994. In his first season at OU, he was named national coach of the year by the Associated Press and the United States Basketball Writers Association after guiding the Sooners to a 23-9 record, including a perfect 15-0 record at home and a return trip to the NCAA tournament that OU had missed the previous two years.

Sampson has the highest winning percentage in Sooner history. He led OU to eight consecutive 20-win seasons and took the team to post-season tournament berths in each of his 11 seasons. The Sooners made it to the Elite Eight in 2003 and the Final Four in 2002. Sampson-coached teams won the Big 12 tournament three times. He holds the best Big 12 Tournament record of 17-6. At OU, he always sported a blue dress shirt in games. It was a lucky charm to fans because the Sooners rarely lost at home. To Sampson's players it was a reminder of the importance of a blue-collar work ethic.

From 2006 to 2008, Sampson was head coach at the University of Indiana, the first Native American coach at the school. After being forced to resign because of alleged NCAA violations, Sampson was hired as an assistant coach of the Milwaukee Bucks of the National Basketball Association.

Life Lessons Taught by Coach Sampson

The foundation for creating a successful basketball team is instilling a culture that promotes overcoming adversity. The basketball season is a journey and the end destination is largely unimportant. Sure, we talked about the end goals all the time, but getting there is where the learning (and fun) takes place. How many times have you seen a coach win it all and a look of melancholy crosses their face? It is the journey that drives us all.

If a student-athlete could handle my conditioning program in September and pre-season practices in October, then they could handle anything in January through March. All my teams had great chemistry because they bonded in the shared experience of overcoming adversity. I hope the young men who played for me look up and realize that life is full of adversity. What separates winners from losers is how people adapt.

Life Lessons Learned from Coach Sampson

Eduardo Najera, a native of Chihuahua, Mexico was recruited to OU in Sampson's first recruiting class. Eduardo spoke little English upon arrival but passed the ACT in English to become eligible and later earned his degree from OU. He is only the second Mexican-born player in the NBA where he has played for four teams since 2000.

Coach Sampson was our toughest critic on the floor and our biggest advocate outside the gymnasium. During my sophomore season, we lost a game in our own "Sooner Invitational" tournament to a small division one school, Murray State. The Racers had a good team in 1997-98, but they were not better than us. We just didn't play hard that night. The following day, Coach had us come watch film before class at 6:00 a.m. We got to the gym and the trainer told us to get dressed for practice.

"Uh oh," we all said collectively. This wasn't good since he had not mentioned practice previously. Following a marathon film session, we came downstairs to find our locker room empty. We had been relocated to the visitors dressing room, a place more befit for "quitters" they said. Down to the floor we went for an hour of running, mostly around the second place silver ball he placed at center court. People were passing out. It was all worth it the following weekend when we beat nationally ranked Arkansas by double digits. The Hogs never saw us coming. There were two lessons learned that day. One, don't quit. Two, we never would have believed we could beat a nationally ranked team if we had not gone through the agony of losing to Murray State. So many people quit in life out of fear of what may lie on the other side.

Courtesy Oklahoma Publishing Company.

BILL SELF

Born in Okmulgee, Oklahoma, Self was Oklahoma High School Basketball Player of the Year at Edmond High School in 1981 and played college basketball at Oklahoma State University for Coach Paul Hansen. After graduating with a business degree from OSU, Self joined Larry Brown's coaching staff at the University of Kansas in 1985. From 1986 to 1993, Self was an assistant coach at OSU under Coaches Leonard Hamilton and Eddie Sutton.

Self's first head coaching job was at Oral Roberts University in 1993. At age 29, he was the youngest head coach in the nation. In his fourth season, he led the Golden Eagles to its first post-season tournament in 15 years. In 1998, Self was hired by cross-town rival, the University of Tulsa, where he spent three seasons, compiling a university-best coaching record of 74-27. In 2000, the Hurricane went 32-5, a single-season record for victories, and made the Elite Eight in the NCAA tournament for the first time.

In 2001, Self moved to the University of Illinois where he coached his squad to a 27-8 record, a share of the Big Ten Conference title, and a number one seed in the NCAA tournament. In three seasons at Illinois, Self led the Fighting Illini to two Big Ten regular-season championships, a Big Ten title, and three consecutive NCAA tournament appearances.

In 2004, Self was hired as head basketball coach at the University of Kansas. In his first five seasons, he won one national championship and four regular-season Big 12 titles. In his first trip to the Final Four in 2008, Self's team won the title. From 2004 to 2009, Self was the winningest coach in NCAA Division I. He has guided his teams to 10 consecutive 20-win seasons.

Self is one of only four coaches in Division I history to lead three teams to the Elite Eight of the NCAA tournament. He was named National Coach of the Year by *The Sporting News* in 2000 and 2009 and by the Associated Press in 2009. He was named Big 12 Coach of the Year in 2006 and 2009.

Courtesy Oklahoma Publishing Company.

Life Lessons Taught by Coach Self

Being part of a basketball team is like being part of a family or business. I encourage players to develop friendships so they can look out for each other and have some-one to lean on. That is an important lesson on campus, but even more important as the young men get married, start a family, and move into jobs and careers.

Good behavior is critical, both as a member of a basketball team and in life. I expect good behavior whether our record is 8-20 or 20-8. Part of winning on the court is being responsible off it—there is a definite correlation. I tell my players to think about consequences of their actions—to consider the bad things that will happen because of poor choices. After all, my player, whether he likes it or not, is a representa-tive of his family, his school, and his state. Good behavior can never be overemphasized.

Life Lessons Learned from Coach Self

From Wagoner, Oklahoma, Dante Swanson is one of the most prolific guards in University of Tulsa history. Coach Self, an emerging national figure in the coach-ing profession, discovered Swanson and recruited him to play at TU.

Coming from AAU and a high school environment, I lacked the small skills that make a big difference at the next level. The thing that I learned from Coach Self was discipline. We needed discipline on and off the court to be successful in life. Sloppy work in the classroom was the same as sloppy play on the court. Coach Self made sure that we had the skills we needed to get the job done—no matter big or small. Athletes need that extra push, especially in the classroom, where relaxing can mean failure.

Courtesy Oklahoma Publishing Company.

JENKS SIMMONS

James Ellington "Jenks" Simmons was known as "Mr. Basketball" in Oklahoma high school sports in the 1940s and 1950s. After graduating from Southwestern Oklahoma Teachers College in 1926, he was rookie of the year for the professional football Cleveland Bulldogs in 1927. He also played for the Providence Steamrollers and helped win the 1928 National Football League championship.

Simmons coached for 27 years at El Reno High School and won five state championships in 1932, 1933, 1946, 1949, and 1953. El Reno won the championship in the Boomer Conference 26 of the 27 years and tied for the crown in the other season. Simmons' 1949 team was undefeated at 24-0.

Simmons' career record at El Reno was 436-144. He also coached basketball and football for six seasons at Northwestern State College in Alva. He was inducted into the Oklahoma Coaches Hall of Fame in 1967 and the Oklahoma Athletics Hall of Fame in 1972.

GRADY SKILLERN

People mattered more to Skillern than victories and he often kept in touch with students for decades after they graduated from his programs. His philosophy was made up of four parts—mental, physical, social, and spiritual.

Skillern compiled a 529-134 basketball coaching record at El Reno High School, Oklahoma City Classen High School, and Central High School in Tulsa before becoming athletic director for Tulsa public schools until his retirement. He won seven state basketball championships.

Because Skillern was the predecessor of Henry Iba at Classen High School, the two coaches had a special relationship. It was on Iba's recommendation that Skillern hired a young Eddie Sutton to coach Central High. Skillern also recommended the hiring of Chuck Bowman as Central's football coach. Bowman later was Oklahoma director of the Fellowship of Christian Athletes for many years.

Former University of Tulsa Athletic Director Glenn Dobbs said about Skillern, "He stood for discipline and love. If you asked him about a person, first he talked about the person's good character traits and then about their ability. He did what he had to do either softly or strongly, but always with a great deal of love."

Courtesy Tulsa Public Schools.

Courtesy Oklahoma Publishing Company.

LARRY STEELE

Steele coached the Oklahoma City Northeast High School girl's team from 1973 to 1988. The Lady Vikings won the state crown in 1979 and were runners-up in 1981.

During the years of debate over transition to girls 5-on-5 play, Steele was a proponent of moving to same style of play as boys. He believed that full court competition for girls would make the game more exciting and teach all girl players to be complete basketball players.

BLOOMER SULLIVAN

Sullivan was named for the Bloomer Green Mountains that surrounded his birthplace in Virginia. His family moved to Ardmore, Oklahoma, where he was introduced to sports. He later was named to the Ardmore High School Half-Century team in 1951.

After high school, Sullivan took a job as student coach at Southeast Normal School, now Southeastern Oklahoma State University. The $30-a-month stipend allowed him to complete college in 1934. He later earned a master's degree from Oklahoma A & M as the first college coach in Oklahoma with an advanced graduate degree.

Sullivan was extremely successful as Southeastern's basketball coach. His record was 662-222 and he coached seven All Americans and 35 All-Conference players. His star player, Jerry Shipp, helped the college to three straight conference championships and played on the United States Olympic team. Another player, Warren Womble, twice coached the American Olympic basketball squad.

The gymnasium at Southeastern in Durant is named for Sullivan who is a member of the NAIA Hall of Fame and the Oklahoma Sports Hall of Fame.

Courtesy Oklahoma Publishing Company.

EDDIE SUTTON

With a college basketball career coaching record of 804-327, Eddie Sutton is one of only seven major college coaches with more than 800 wins. He was born in Kansas but came to Oklahoma State University to play basketball under Coach Henry Iba.

After college graduation, Sutton was an assistant coach at OSU for one year before coaching basketball at Central High School in Tulsa for seven years. He coached for three years at Southern Idaho Junior College before launching a superb major college coaching career at Creighton University in 1969.

In 1974, Sutton began an 11-year stint as men's basketball coach at the University of Arkansas. He took the Razorbacks to nine NCAA tournaments and the Final Four in 1978. In 1985, he assumed the head coaching job at the University of Kentucky.

After four seasons at Kentucky, Sutton returned to his alma mater, OSU, to revive its storied basketball program. In 17 seasons under Sutton, the Cowboys reached the postseason 14 times, had 13 appearances in the NCAA Tournament, and two trips to the Final Four. He is the second-winningest coach in OSU basketball history, second only to his mentor, Henry Iba.

Sutton had 798 wins when he resigned as OSU basketball coach in 2006. He came out of retirement to temporarily coach the University of San Francisco in 2007 and reached the 800-win plateau.

In his career, Sutton won five Southwest Conference regular season championships, one Southeast Conference championship, two Big Eight Conference championships, and won the Big 12 Conference regular season crown in 2004 and the Big 12 Tournament in 2005. He was the Associated Press National Coach of the Year in 1978 and 1986, the Southwest Conference Coach of the Year four times, Big 12 Coach of the Year twice, and SEC and Big Eight Coach of the Year once each.

Courtesy Oklahoma Publishing Company.

Sutton was the first coach to take four schools to the NCAA Tournament. He is among the elite by taking two schools, Arkansas and OSU, to the Final Four. On January 15, 2005, the court at Gallagher-Iba Arena at OSU was officially renamed Eddie Sutton Court. Sutton is a member of the Oklahoma Sports Hall of Fame.

Life Lessons Taught by Coach Sutton

I always considered myself a teacher. Early in my coaching career, I figured out that life was like a basketball season—some days you win, some days you lose. My job as a teacher and coach was to teach kids how to live a successful life, not just be a basketball star.

Teaching can be done in many ways. During a game, it might take the form of dramatically emphasizing a mistake that a player made. Young men will take intense criticism if they know you love them. I told players, "Don't listen to the tone of my voice, listen to what I am telling you. Teaching also includes serious instruction and even joking around at practice, making the players feel good about themselves.

At the end of the day, I wanted the young men I coached to play great basketball and represent Oklahoma State University in a class manner. I love to read about the success of my former players, not just in basketball, but what they do for their families and communities, how they give back to their university and state. I am honored to play a minor role in shaping their lives.

Life Lessons Learned from Coach Sutton

Desmond Mason was one of the great players to wear a Cowboy uniform. Originally from Waxahachie, Texas, Desmond was the jewel of a highly recruited 1996 OSU class that followed the Final Four team of 1995. Desmond was known as an athletic forward with undeveloped potential as a basketball player. Desmond went on to play in the NBA for the Seattle, New Orleans, Milwaukee, Oklahoma City, and Sacramento.

Our first public practice was called the Eddie Sutton Baseline Bash and everyone was excited to see one of the top recruiting classes in the country hit the floor. Gallagher-Iba Arena was completely packed and the student section was going crazy. We started with a three man weave drill and I got the ball on the wing went up to dunk it. The next thing I knew, I had shattered the backboard. The shattered glass covered the floor and I had small cuts, but the entire student section stormed the court to pick up pieces as memorabilia. For the next week I autographed big and small pieces of glass for students that were in my classes.

But, the day after the bash is when I received my life lesson from Coach Sutton. We were having a team practice and things were going well until I got into a "disagreement" with a senior teammate. Very quickly Coach Sutton stood up from the bleachers and told me to shut my mouth. Coach went on to share that that senior had played in Final Four of the NCAA tournament with great success and had made his mark in college basketball. He also told me that I hadn't accomplished anything at this level, and just because I broke a backboard doesn't make me a basketball player. His final words to me before he told me to count every

Scott Sutton, right, with his brother, former OSU men's basketball coach Sean Sutton. *Courtesy Oklahoma Publishing Company.*

SCOTT SUTTON

Sutton, born in Nebraska, became head men's basketball coach at Oral Roberts University in 1999. The younger son of legendary coach Eddie Sutton, Scott was the first ORU coach since Ken Trickey to reach the NCAA tournament. He was hired at ORU as an assistant to Coach Bill Self.

In his first ten years at ORU, Sutton led the Golden Eagles to four regular-season conference titles, averaged more than 18 wins per season, and made three consecutive NCAA tournaments from 2006 to 2008. He is second to Trickey in all-time victories at ORU.

Sutton was named Summit League Coach of the Year in 2008.

---

step in Gallagher Iba Arena was, "If you argue with a senior again I'll run you back to Waxahachie, Texas."

That was my welcome to Oklahoma State University. That incident taught me to respect everyone regardless of their age. Whether they're younger than you or older than you, everyone should be respected. I had always respected my elders, but the younger someone was, the less respect I gave in return. So the one of many lessons I've taken from Coach Sutton, and used every day since, is to respect everyone regardless of race, religion, sex or age.

Courtesy Oklahoma Publishing Company.

If you give 100% all of the time, somehow things will work out in the end.

Bertha Teague

BERTHA TEAGUE

Bertha Frank Teague built a basketball dynasty at Byng High School during a 43-year coaching career. Born in Missouri, she graduated from high school in Amity, Arkansas, and earned a degree at Oklahoma A & M. Even before she completed college, she and her husband were hired in 1927 to teach at the small, rural school at Byng, a few miles north of Ada, Oklahoma.

Teague was a first grade teacher, and although she had never coached basketball, became the high school girls' coach. For the next several decades, she modernized the sport in Oklahoma and nationally. She established the first girls' basketball clinic in the Southwest.

Teague's teams won eight state championships, 22 regional titles, 27 district titles, and 38 conference championships. Byng made 22 state tournaments, had five undefeated seasons, and won 98 consecutive games from 1936 to 1938. Her career won-loss record was an improbable 1,136-116 in 43 years.

Teague's legacy is lasting and her influence is still felt in high school sports. Many honors have been bestowed upon her—she is a member of every hall of fame for which she is eligible. She is the only woman coach in the Naismith Memorial Basketball Hall of Fame. She has been inducted into the Oklahoma Sports Hall of Fame, the National Federation of State High Schools Hall of Fame, the Oklahoma State University Alumni Association Hall of Fame, the Oklahoma Girls Basketball Coaches Association Hall of Fame, and is the only woman in the Missouri Basketball Hall of Fame.

Courtesy Oklahoma Publishing Company.

KEN TRICKEY

In the early 1970s, Trickey took an Oral Roberts University basketball program in its infancy and turned it into a powerhouse. The Titans rose from NAIA status into a team that narrowly missed making the NCAA Final Four. In 1974, Trickey led ORU to the Midwest Regional final before losing to Kansas in overtime.

Trickey had two stints at ORU and also coached at Iowa State, Middle Tennessee, and Oklahoma City University. He was a high school coach in Illinois, Tennessee, and in Muskogee, Oklahoma. In 2003, at age 69, he came out of retirement to coach high school basketball at Muskogee.

Courtesy Oklahoma Publishing Company.

BILLY TUBBS

In 31 years of coaching, Billy Tubbs posed a 641-340 record in college basketball. He was born in Tulsa, Oklahoma, and graduated from Lamar University in Texas. He coached men's basketball at Lamar from 1976 to 1980 when he became coach at the University of Oklahoma.

At OU, Tubbs created excitement for Sooner fans with "Billy ball," a display of offensive power. Tubbs was known for high scoring offense and full court press defense.

In 1994, Tubbs moved to the men's basketball program at Texas Christian University. In 2002, he returned to Lamar and coached until 2006. He became the ninth coach in NCAA history to record 100 wins at three different schools. He also was the 28th coach in Division I history to record 600 wins.

Tubbs took 12 teams to NCAA Tournament appearances and six teams to the NIT. He won eight conference championships and had 18 20-win seasons.

LIFE LESSONS TAUGHT BY COACH TUBBS

Never hold grudges and dwell on things of the past. You can learn from mistakes and try to improve from past experiences, positive and negative, but you make another critical mistake if you keep thinking about the past. If people on the other side of the fence want to continue to dwell on last year, that's their problem. But for my players and me, we're always looking forward.

I always wanted my players to be confident that they could win on any court against any team. I also wanted them to win in life, in business, in a profession, or as a husband or father. I did not want them to be intimidated on the basketball court or in their future lives. The only way to not be intimidated is to be confident in your abilities and play to win. Don't let the opinions of your competitors keep you from doing your best.

LIFE LESSONS LEARNED FROM COACH TUBBS

Kermit Holmes played basketball for OU from 1989 to 1991 for Billy Tubbs. He earned team MVP honors in 1991 after averaging 14.8 points per game and leading the team in rebounding at 9.3 per game. Additionally, Holmes helped Oklahoma post a two-year record of 47-20. The 1990 Sooners reached the second round of the NCAA Tournament and the 1991 squad advanced to the championship game of the National Invitation Tournament (NIT) at Madison Square Garden in New York City.

I'm fortunate because I've gotten to know Billy both as a coach, friend and boss. I was recruited to play for him, got to know him on a personal level after OU while I played professionally, and then had the opportunity to work for him at Lamar.

Coach Tubbs wanted us to have fun. Former players always talk about how coaches were like "fathers" to them. Billy wasn't a father figure to me. He was my coach. I learned how to play the game at a high level while at OU and I learned how to have fun. Basketball is a game that should be enjoyed and too often college athletes forget to enjoy the game. With Billy, we played ball. It was an exciting style and we loved it and the fans loved it. Billy taught us to never take ourselves too seriously. Oh, and to shoot if we were open and to win.

No Matter How Bad the Officiating

One of the most memorable moments in Oklahoma basketball history occurred on February 9, 1989, at Lloyd Noble Center on the OU campus in Norman. A record crowd was watching No. 3 Missouri play No. 5 OU in an ESPN nationally-televised Thursday night game.

Missouri jumped out to a 23-8 lead in the first five minutes. OU Coach Billy Tubbs had one technical foul when another controversial call 40 seconds later set the crowd to booing and several patrons threw debris onto the court.

Tubbs calmly walked to the public address announcer to quiet the crowd. In an unforgettable announcement, Tubbs said, "Regardless of how terrible the officiating is, please don't throw things onto the floor." Official Ed Hightower immediately assessed Tubbs his second technical. OU rallied and won the game.

Years later, Tubbs and Hightower disagree on what happened. Tubbs said Hightower asked him to speak to the crowd. Hightower's memory is that Tubbs asked for the microphone. Tubbs said, "I was commanded to do it. I might have done a poor job of what they asked me to do, but I have a bad habit of being very truthful."

Three days later, OU hosted No. 1 Arizona. Wildcats Coach Lute Olson walked past public address announcer Mike Treps and playfully asked, "Is that working OK? You need Billy to do a mike check?"

JOHNNIE WILLIAMS

Williams died in 2002 just six weeks after one of his AAU teams won one of his dozens of championship trophies. In the late 1950s, Williams began coaching summer basketball teams. AAU President Bobby Dodd said, "Johnnie got into summer basketball long before sponsorships paid the bills. He did it with a love for how he could help young athletes." OSU star Leroy Combs, who played for Williams, said, "Many of his players came from impoverished areas and broken homes. They needed rides to practice and money for trips. Whatever they needed, Coach got it for them. If you needed him, he was always there."

Williams was born in Geary, Oklahoma, and played at Oklahoma Christian College. In more than five decades, Williams coached some of the best players Oklahoma has ever seen, including Wayman Tisdale, Richard Dumas, Byron Houston, and Mark and Brent Price. Photographs of his players, numbering in the hundreds, covered one wall of his living room. He won literally dozens of championships.

To honor Williams' contribution, the Municipal Gymnasium in Oklahoma City has been named for him.

Courtesy Oklahoma Publishing Company.

Courtesy Oklahoma Publishing Company.

RANKIN WILLIAMS

Williams's life is closely interwoven with the story of Southwestern Oklahoma State University (SWOSU) in Weatherford. His father, a member of the Oklahoma territorial legislature, owned the land that is now occupied by part of the university. In high school in Weatherford, Williams was one of Oklahoma's best athletes and continued his success in baseball, basketball, and track in college at SWOSU. He held the state college record in both high and low hurdles for many years.

When the SWOSU basketball coach left in the middle of the season in 1923, Williams took over the team as a player-coach. For the next 42 years, he coached every major and minor sport the school offered. He won 19 consecutive conference championships and logged 435 wins as a basketball coach. At SWOSU, Williams guided his teams to eight conference championships. Before he retired, he became the first college coach to collect more than 1,000 wins in all sports.

Williams is a member of the NAIA Hall of Fame, the Oklahoma Athletic Hall of Fame, the Helms Foundation Hall of Fame, and the NAIA Basketball Hall of Fame.

WARREN WOMBLE

Born in Durant, Womble played basketball at Southeastern State College, now Southeastern Oklahoma State University, on a team that reached the quarterfinals of the national AAU tournament in 1948.

Womble was a legendary coach in the National Industrial Basketball League and was the first director of the league. For ten years, from 1951 to 1960, he coached the league's Peoria Caterpillars. In five of those seasons, he won the national Amateur Athletic Union championship.

Womble coached the United States Olympic basketball team three times, in 1952, as head coach, and in 1956 and 1960, as assistant coach. The 1952 American team defeated the Soviet Union, 36-25, to win the gold medal. Two years later, Womble coached the American gold medal team in international basketball competition and led the first American team to tour the Soviet Union.

Courtesy Oklahoma Sports Hall of Fame.

In the1960 summer Olympics in Rome, Italy, Womble coached future Hall of Famers Jerry West, Oscar Robertson, Walt Bellamy, and Jerry Lucas. The Americans beat Brazil 90-36 for the gold medal. Womble is a member of the Helms Foundation Hall of Fame and the Oklahoma Athletic Hall of Fame.

Courtesy Northeastern Oklahoma A&M College.

DIXIE WOODALL

A member of the Women's Basketball Hall of Fame, Dixie Woodall was a three-time AAU All-American with the Raytown Piperettes. She played on the Nashville Business College 1960 AAU national champion team, earned a silver medal as a member of the American squad at the 1967 Pan American Games, and represented the United States on teams that toured South America in 1965.

Woodall was an assistant coach for the United States team that won a silver medal at the 1977 World University Games in Bulgaria and has coached several American women's teams in international competition.

Woodall was women's basketball coach at Seminole Junior College for ten seasons. She won the national junior college championship in 1976 with runner-up finishes in 1975 and 1977. In 1977, she moved to Oral Roberts University where she coached women's basketball for four seasons. In 1978, she produced ORU's first female All-American, Rhonda Penquite. Woodall's career record was 390-97. She was inducted into the Women's Basketball Hall of Fame in 2005.

Courtesy Oklahoma Publishing Company.

JIM WOOLRIDGE

A native of Oklahoma City, Woolridge played on Putnam City High School's Class 4A state basketball championship team in 1972. He earned a bachelor's degree from Louisiana Tech University and a master's degree from East Central University.

Woolridge began his head coaching career at Central Missouri State University in 1985. After six seasons at Central Missouri, he coached three years at Texas State University and four years at Louisiana Tech. He was an assistant coach for the Chicago Bulls from 1998 to 2000 before he returned to the college ranks at Kansas State University where he coached the Wildcat men basketball team for six years. In 2007, he was named head coach at the University of California-Riverside.

OTHER
NOTABLE COACHES

The following coaches are not featured in the previous section, but nevertheless have contributed greatly to the history of basketball in Oklahoma.

JERRY BELTON won six boys state championships at Boynton.

STEVE BONTRAGER, a native of Iowa, played college basketball at Oral Roberts University. In 1992, he coached the Tulsa Zone in the professional Continental Basketball Association and was a long-time youth and professional instructor of basketball in Tulsa.

CHET BRYAN was one of the state's best high school basketball coaches at Norman, winning four state titles in 14 years. He then moved to baseball and made a name for himself at OSU, winning the Big Eight baseball title in 13 seasons.

DAVE BLISS was a major college coach for 28 seasons. His first head coaching job was at Oklahoma from 1975 to 1980. He coached eight years at Southern Methodist University, 11 seasons at the University of New Mexico, and four years at Baylor University.

SCOTT BROOKS is the head coach of the NBA Oklahoma City Thunder. He was a collegiate star at the University of California-Irvine. After graduation, he played ten seasons in the NBA. After working as an assistant coach for the Sacramento Kings and Denver Nuggets, Brooks became assistant coach for the Oklahoma City Thunder. In December, 2008, he became interim coach for the Thunder and was elevated to head coach for the 2009 season.

KURT BUDKE became the women's basketball coach at Oklahoma State University in 2006. He arrived at OSU from Louisiana Tech University where he was named Western Athletic Conference coach of the year in 2003. He was twice named the national coach of the year by the National Junior College Athletic Association (NJCAA) and is the youngest coach ever inducted into the NJCAA Hall of Fame.

JEFF CAPEL is the head men's basketball coach at the University of Oklahoma. After a stellar career as a starting guard for the Duke University basketball team, Capel's first head coaching job was at Virginia Commonwealth University in 2002. At age 27, he was the youngest head coach in Division I of the NCAA. He was named head basketball coach at OU in 2006.

FRANKLIN "CAPPY" CAPPON played football and basketball at Phillips University in Enid, Oklahoma. He was a legendary men's basketball coach at the University of Kansas, the University of Michigan, and Princeton University from 1926 to 1961. His final 23 years were at Princeton. He is a member of the Helms Foundation College Basketball Hall of Fame.

P.J. CARLESIMO was the first head coach of the Oklahoma City Thunder when the NBA came to Oklahoma City in 2008. He had a super successful college coaching career at Seton Hall University where he was named basketball coach of the century. He was hired by the Seattle Supersonics as head coach in 2007 and moved with the team when the franchise relocated in Oklahoma City. He was released by the Thunder in November, 2008.

TRAVIS FORD is the men's basketball coach at Oklahoma State University. He previously coached at Eastern Kentucky University and the University of Massachusetts. He became head coach at OSU in 2008 and took the Cowboys to their first NCAA tournament since 2005.

TOMMY GRIFFIN won two state boys high school championships at John Marshall High School. He is the father of OU stars Blake and Taylor Griffin.

LEONARD HAMILTON was men's coach at Oklahoma State University from 1986 to 1990. He then coached basketball at the University of Miami, Florida, for 10 years, for the NBA Washington Wizards for one season, and has been the men's coach at Florida State University since 2002.

TOM HEIDEBRECHT won five girls state championships at Hydro, Fort Towson, and Washita Heights.

BRUCE HOBGOOD coached the Lomega girls to five state championships.

BOB HOFFMAN coached at several levels of basketball, at Oklahoma Baptist University, as an assistant at OU, in the NBA, and at Pan American University.

MOE IBA, the son of Henry P. Iba, graduated from Oklahoma State University in 1962. He was head men's basketball coach at the University of Memphis for four years, the University of Nebraska for five seasons, and at Texas Christian University from 1986 to 1994.

JIM KNAPP won five state boys championships at Smithville and New Lima

GARY LOOOPER won five boys state championships at Purcell and Oklahoma City McGuinness.

JOHN MACLEOD was men's basketball coach at the University of Oklahoma from 1967 to 1974. He also coached collegiately at Notre Dame University from 1991 to 1999. He was a head coach for 16 years in the NBA for the Phoenix Suns, New York Knicks, and Dallas Mavericks.

WAYNE MERRIMAN coached at Colbert for 30 of his 34 years and led the boys and girls teams to five state championships.

JOHN PHILLIPS was a successful coach at the University of Tulsa and several high schools.

BURL PLUNKETT coached the OU women for three seasons from 1994 to 1996, leading the team to the Women's NIT championship in 1994. During his longtime high school coaching career at Valliant and Byng, he won 35 district championships and three girls state titles. Plunkett died in 2008.

DAVID SANDERS won six state championships in girls basketball at Stigler and Cheyenne.

TERRY SCOTT became men's basketball coach at Muskogee High School in 2009 after 22 years at Central High School in Tulsa. Scott led Central to three state championships.

TUBBY SMITH coached men's basketball at the University of Tulsa from 1991 to 1995. He later coached at the University of Kentucky for ten seasons. He was named head men's basketball coach at the University of Minnesota in 2007.

SEAN SUTTON, the son of Eddie Sutton, played basketball under his father at the University of Kentucky and Oklahoma State University. He followed his father as head men's coach at OSU in 2006. He served in that position until early in 2008.

CHARLENE THOMAS-SWINSON became head women's basketball coach at the University of Tulsa in 2005 after a long career as an assistant coach at Auburn, Florida, and Columbia Union. She is the first coach in TU women's basketball history to win a conference championship and take the women's team to the NCAA tournament.

GERALD TUCKER was the head coach of the 1956 United States Olympic basketball team that won the gold medal. He was a star center at the University of Oklahoma and was twice named a Helms Foundation All American. In 1947, he was the Helms Foundation Player of the Year. He later played for and coached the Bartlesville Phillips 66ers of the National Industrial Basketball League. He won the AAU national championship in 1955.

DOUG WOJCIK became men's basketball coach at the University of Tulsa in 2005. In his first five seasons, Wojcik surpassed Tubby Smith and Bill Self in career wins and led the Golden Hurricane to three consecutive 20-win seasons for the first time in history.

THE GREATEST OKLAHOMA BASKETBALL TEAMS

These teams were selected by sportswriters at *The Oklahoman* in 2007 as part of Oklahoma's centennial celebration.

1945 Oklahoma State University men—It was Bob Kurland's junior year and the Cowboys beat New York University 49-45 to win the national championship. The NCAA Tournament received a boost in status when the Cowboys then beat NIT champion DePaul University in a historic American Red Cross benefit game.

1972 Putnam City High School boys—The Pirates were led by Alvan Adams and future college coaches Darrell Johnson and Jim Wooldridge who dominated to win 26 games against no losses. It was the last time a big-school state champion went unbeaten.

1988 University of Oklahoma men—Fans and sportswriters knew OU was the best team in the land despite an 83-79 loss to Kansas in the NCAA national championship game in Kansas City. The Sooners average more than 102 points per game. Stacey King and Harvey Grant were named All-Americans, although Mookie Blaylock was perhaps the best player on the team.

1995 Tulsa Washington High School boys—An incredible Hornets team that posted a 26-1 record, led by future NBA players Derrick (Etan) Thomas and Ryan Humphrey and future professional football star R.W. McQuarters.

2002 University of Oklahoma women—The Sooner women reached the NCAA title game and played well against the University of Connecticut tea. OU was led by All-American Stacey Dales and LaNeishea Caufield.

1933 DX-Oilers AAU—Oklahoma had one of the strongest AAU programs in the nation in the 1920s and 1930s, but did not win a national championship until Bart Carlton and Chuck Hyatt starred in a finals victory over a team from Chicago, Illinois.

1996 Indianola High School girls—Krista Ragan led the Class 2A state championship with a 30-1 record, their only loss to Norman that won the Class 6A title. Indianola also beat Norman that year.

1996 Norman High School girls—Sherri Coale coached her Tigers to a state championship in the state's highest class with a 27-1 record, their only loss to Indianola. The team was led by future college stars Sara Dimson and Stacy Hansmeyer.

1978 New Lima High School boys—With a 31-0 record, the Class B state champions also won the Tournament of Champions, beating Tulsa Washington. Seniors Eddie Louie and George Allen finished their careers at New Lima with two state championships and a 113-10 record.

1940 Phillips 66ers—Chuck Hyatt, who had starred in the 1933 AAU tournament, coached the 66ers to the first of 11 national AAU championships. Led by Grady Lewis, Joe Fortenberry, and Don Lockhard, the 66ers beat the defending champion Denver Nuggets in the title game.

1932 Presbyterian College women—The college in Durant won the national AAU title in women's basketball. Doll Harris scored 19 points in the finals against the Dallas Golden Cyclones.

2004 Oklahoma State University men—Perhaps Eddie Sutton's best team. Tony Allen and John Lucas were named the Big 12 Conference co-players of the year. The Cowboys won 21 of their final 22 games before a two point upset loss to Georgia Tech University in the Final Four.

1998 Ada High School girls—Future OU stars Caton Hill and LaNeishea Caufield led Ada to the Class 5A title with a 24-1 record.

1946 Oklahoma State University men—The first college team to repeat as national champions beat the University of North Carolina in the finals. Bob Kurland also repeated as an All-American.

1979 Star Spencer High School boys—It was the fourth consecutive state title. Future OSU star Leroy Combs and Kenneth Orange led the 28-0 team.

1950 Grainola High School girls—The small high school in Osage County had only 14 students, but nine girls played basketball and won the Class B state championship. Three months after the championship, the school was closed.

1947 University of Oklahoma men—Coach Bruce Drake won the Big Six Conference title and reached the national championship game where the Sooners lost to Bob Cousy and Holy Cross University. All-American Gerald Tucker was the OU star.

1982 Southwestern Oklahoma State University women—Freshman Kelli Litsch and rookie head coach John Loftin led Southwestern to its first of five NAIA national championships in a nine-year span with a 34-0 record. The team won its three games in the national tournament by a combined 83 points.

1938 Byng High School girls—Coach Bertha Teague won her third consecutive state championship and moved the team's winning streak to 90, eventually reaching 98 the following season.

1949 El Reno High School boys—At 24-0, Coach Jenks Simmons led the team to a state championship, led by Leroy Bacher, Kendall Sheets, and Gerald Stockton.

1995 Oklahoma State University men—Bryant "Big Country" Reeves outplayed future NBA stars Antonio McDyess, Tim Duncan, and Marcus Camby as the Cowboys stormed to the Final Four.

1992 Oklahoma City University men—The Chiefs sported a 38-0 record and won its first national championship since 1965. All-Americans Eric Manuel and Smokey McCovery led the team.

1979 Colbert High School girls—With a perfect 32-0 record, star forwards Judy Thomas and Anita Lyons completed their high school career with three state championships, a triple-overtime loss in another state title, and a 131-7 overall record.

2002 University of Oklahoma men—Kelvin Sampson led the Sooners in winning 16 of their final 17 games before an upset loss to the University of Indiana in the Final Four. Hollis Price was named All American.

1940 Nuyaka High School boys—The now-consolidated Oklahoma County high school won its second straight Class C title and beat eventual Class A champion Ada by 13 points in a special holiday match game.

1928 University of Oklahoma men—The Sooners were 18-0. Vic Holt was an All American. His teammates included future OU coach Bruce Drake and Tom Churchill.

1966 Oklahoma Baptist University men—The Bison, led by All-American Al Tucker and coached by Bob Bass, won the first NAIA national championship by an Oklahoma school.

1974 Oral Roberts University men—The Golden Eagles reached the brink of the Final Four, just nine years after the school opened. ORU lost to Kansas by three points in the Midwest Regional final.

1996 John Marshall High School boys—With a perfect 28-0 record, John Marshall won the state championship in the state's highest class.

1949 Oklahoma State University men—Coach Henry Iba played for his third national title in five years but lost by ten points to the University of Kentucky in the finals. Bob Harris and J.L. Parks made All American.

1964 Mangum High School girls—The Mangum girls, led by Grett Hogan, won their second consecutive Class A state championship and extended their winning streak to 59 games.

1981 University of Tulsa men—With a 26-7 record, Coach Nolan Richardson won the NIT title over Syracuse University in overtime. At that time, the NIT was considered a major force in college basketball.

1992 Hammon High School boys—Twins Ryan and Damon Minor led Hammon to a second consecutive state championship in Class B. Ryan scored a record 105 points in three state tournament games. Both brothers went on to OU and played basketball and baseball.

1985 University of Oklahoma men—Wayman Tisdale ended his career with a two point loss to Memphis State University in the regional final for Coach Billy Tubbs. OU was 31-6.

1974 Deer Creek High School boys—Don Dodd coached his team to a victory over all in-state opponents with a record of 32-1. Deer Creek beat two-time defending Class B champion Sasakwa by ten points in the state semifinal.

2002 Woodward High School girls—Future University of Texas star Kala Bowers led the team to a 26-1 record and the state championship in Class 5A.

1980 Cameron University men—Andre King and Leroy Jackson led the Aggies to a 36-3 record and the NAIA national title.

1951 Oklahoma State University men—Coach Henry Iba made the Final Four for the fourth time in seven years. The team had a 29-6 record with two of the losses coming in the Final Four against Kansas State in the semifinals and Illinois in the third-place game.

1966 Inola High School boys—The team had a perfect record until being upset by Stroud in the Class B semifinals. Although Inola did not win the state crown, they finished the season 32-1 with wins over three big schools, Tulsa Memorial, Tulsa East Central, and Oklahoma City Northeast, in the Tournament of Champions.

1979 University of Oklahoma men—This team was OU's only conference champion between 1949 and 1984. The Sooners reached the Sweet Sixteen where they lost to Larry Bird and Indiana State University.

1994 University of Tulsa men—Gary Collier and Shea Steals starred on Coach Tubby Smith's team that upset UCLA and OSU in the NCAA tournament at the Myriad Convention Center in Oklahoma City.

MEMBERS OF THE GIRLS BASKETBALL COACHES ASSOCIATION HALL OF FAME

John L. Allison
Clyde Archer
Jack Barnett
Milburn Barton
Larry Bennett
Maholon P. "Doc" Bennett
Carol Bond-Parker
Glen Brawley
Kenneth R. Brixley
Jim Brown
Benny Burnett
Charles Burnett
Dennis Campbell
Lloyd Cargill
Nadiene Carpenter
Geraldine Carrick
Jack Carter
Don Chancellor
Calvin Cleveland
Clifton Collins
Diwayne Collins
Lloyd Conover
Mike Cook
Walter Cooper
Clifton Cotton
Jack Cox
Jim Crabb
Johnny Crabb
Joe Cribb
J. T. Dixon
Truman Dixon
M.K. Derrick
Karren Edgar-Knight
Neal Edwards
Pat Elder
Hermon Emerson
Larry Erwin
Dennis Fine

W.L. Findley
Eldon Flinn
J.D. Flowers
Richard Flud
Whitey Ford
Jimmy Freeman
Howard Gautier
Truman Gilchrist
James C. Goddard
Freddie Gordon
Ronnie Hales
Charles K. Heatly
Bob Helmuth
Joe Paul Hemphill
Jerry Henderson
Lee Henderson
W.D. Hibler
Rav Hogan
L.R. Holley
Delbert Holt
Walt Huffman
Alan Hull
Kenneth Hull
Jim Hurd
Garvin Issacs
Darrell James
Pete Jayroe
Bill Johnson
Omega Johnson
Rick Johnson
Harold Jones
W.C "Dub" Jordan
T. Phil Keirl
Jim Keith
John Kingery
Austin Lindley
Phil Landrum
Jack Lorenz

Mike Maddox
Monte Madewell
Jeff Maloy
Jo Mann
John Maxwell
J.T. Mayfield
Lawernce McCullah
Ron McGuire
Wayne Merryman
Danny Moore
Glenn Moore
Shelby Morgan
Wayne Morgan
Raymond Moss
Bill Mulkey
Kenneth Murphy
Don Muse
Cherie Myers
John Nobles
Jack Ogle
Scott Ousley
Nelson Peach
Jim Peck
Garland Pennington
Bob Pigg
Burl Plunkett
Paul Pool
Guv Powers
Jerry Pugh
Connie Ramsey
Larry Rehl
Sam Rehl
Sherman Southard
Mike Tucker
Jack Wilson
Randy Woolbright
Ivan Wooton

BASKETBALL COACHES IN THE OKLAHOMA COACHES ASSOCIATION HALL OF FAME

Harold Aldridge
Bill Allen
Jerry Anderson
Perry Anderson
Jerry Belton
Doc Bennett
Bob Brumley
Chet Bryan
Lloyd Conover
Walter Cooper
Lawrence Cudjoe
Gene Davis
Harley Day
Leon Dixon
Truman Dixon
Jack Dobbins
Doug Dugger
Dusty Eby
Leroy Estes
Joe Gilbert
C.C. Gillespie
Chris Gillespie
Virgil Granthan
Tommy Griffin
Roy Grissom
Bill Grove
J.V. Haney
Cecil Hankins
Clester Harrington
Jerry Havens
Charles Heatly

W.D. Hibler
Ray Hogan
Joe Holladay
Henry Iba
Pete Jayroe
Jerry Jobe
Claude Kedy
Jim Keith
Jim Knapp
Jim Koch
Bill Koller
Paul Landrith
Joe Laughlin
Abe Lemons
Martin Loper
Willis Mackey
Max Marquardt
Leroy Matthews
Mickey McBride
Wayne Merryman
Raymond Miller
Carl Nick
Scott Ousley
Claude Overton
Eldon Payne
Nelson Peach
Jimmy Peck
Luther Pegues
John Phillips
Don Piccolo
Bobby Pigg

Harold Piper
M.W. Potts
John Pratt
Nathaniel Quinn
W.W. Raper
Howard Ray
Jack Ray
Sam Rehl
John Rind
Gene Robbins
Byron Roberts
Henry Roland
Carl Scott
Joe Shoulders
Jenks Simmons
Alan Simpson
Grady Skillern
Leo Smallwood
Kenneth Sooter
Alex Springs
Chuck Stephens
Marvin Stokes
Bloomer Sullivan
Sam Taylor
Bertha Teague
Don Van Pool
Bailey Van Zant
Terry West
Woodrow West
Vernon Yates

BASKETBALL COACHES IN THE OKLAHOMA SPORTS HALL OF FAME

Bob Bass   Bruce Drake   Zip Gayles

Paul Hansen   Don Haskins   Henry Iba

Abe Lemons   Jenks Simmons   Bloomer Sullivan

Eddie Sutton   Bertha Teague   Billy Tubbs

INDEX